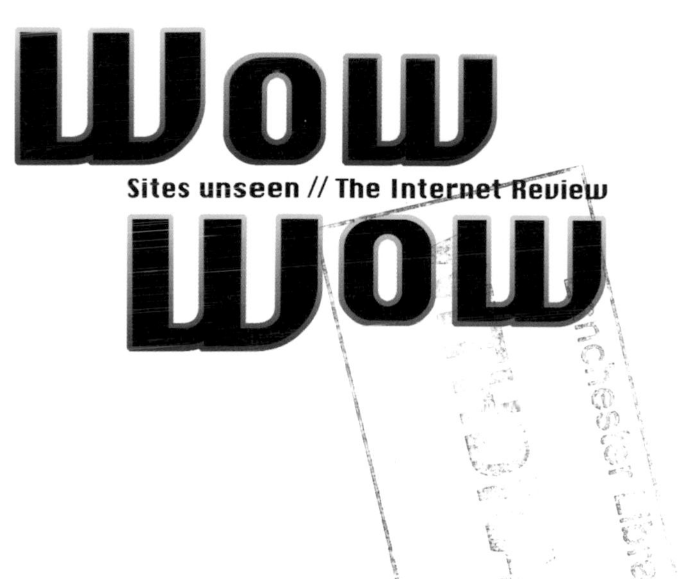

Wow

Sites unseen // The Internet Review

Wow

Laurence King

STRIDE®
WWW.STRIDE-ON.COM
14:23:17 18 FEB 00
BLN52°30'N 13°22'W

Contents

CLUBS

ART

NASTY

SILLY

EARTH

HOBBIES

RUDE

Contributors

Karen Alexander has taught extensively about independent film and video. She works for the and is currently a member of the Arts Council's Visual Arts Panel. (p99)

Stephen Bayley Writer and design consultant. Long ago, he was to have been responsible for filling the Millennium Dome – but he knows a shambles when he sees one and found some other things to get on with. (p54–55)

Lewis Blackwell Creative and brand director of *gettyone*, a channel of Getty Images. He is also the author of several bestselling books on communication, and lectures and consults internationally. (p98)

Mick Brown Journalist for the *Telegraph* magazine, and the author of four books, the most recent a user's guide to the cult film *Performance*. (p16–17)

Patrick Burgoyne Editor of *Creative Review* magazine. (p91–93)

Kate Bush Senior programmer at The Photographers' Gallery, London. (p132–134)

Jess Cartner-Morley Deputy fashion editor of *The Guardian*, she bonded with the web during a previous life as a researcher. (p74–77)

Billy Childish has published thirty collections of his poetry and two novels. He continues to live and paint in his home town of Chatham. (p80–83)

Nick Compton Freelance journalist and writer-at-large for *Arena* magazine. He has also written for *The Face*, *Sky*, *Elle* and *The Sunday Times*. (p121–123)

Harry Crabbe (Jnr) is currently in development. (p30–31)

Deirdre Crowley Multi-media prospector. (p94–97)

Liz Farrelly Writer/editor/decoder of popular culture. (p28–29)

Naoko Hasegawa Japanese freelance design journalist. Previously she was assistant editor of *Designer's Workshop* magazine. (p112–113)

Philip Hoare has written about Stephen Tennant, Noël Coward and Oscar Wilde. His next book, about a military hospital, will be published by Fourth Estate. (p50–53)

Will Hobson Translator and contributing editor to *Granta* magazine. (p142–125)

Michael Hogan Editor of *Sky* magazine. He has also written for *Elle* and *J17*. (p70–71)

Sebastian Horsley Painter, writer and failed suicide. (p146–149)

Oliver Horton Editor of *fw* magazine and a contributing editor to *FHM Collections*. He also writes for *Arena*, *Sky* and *Arena Homme Plus*. (p72–73)

Robin Hunt Creative director of *arehaus*, a new media consultancy. Previously head of New Media at *The Guardian* and a launch editor of *Wired UK*. He is a visiting professor in informatics at City University, London and is writing a book about retail. (p48)

Susan Irvine is a journalist who lives in London. (p12–15)

Mark Irving Writes on the arts, architecture and design for *The Guardian*, *The Independent on Sunday*, *The Express*, *Blueprint* and is author (with Marcus Field) of *Lofts*, an examination of the bohemian origins of life in the inner city. (p36–37)

Emily King Design historian and writer. (p20–23)

Medlar Lucan Aesthete, restaurateur and cabaret artiste, is the author (with Durian Gray) of *The Decadent Cookbook, The Decadent Gardener* and – coming soon – *The Decadent Traveller*. (p33–35)

Serena Mackesy is a freelance journalist. Her first novel, *The Temp*, was published in October 1999. (p49)

Andrew Marshall Washington based bureau chief for *The Independent*, writes frequently about technology, culture and politics in the USA. (p106–109, 124–125)

Alex Martin Freelance writer based in Oxford, has written books on history, literature, gardening and food. New work includes a guide to contemporary Britain and a book for the National Gallery in London. He also edits a series for the publisher Dedalus on the history of outrageous behaviour. (p84–85)

Andy Martin Author of *Walking on Water*, used to be the best surfer in Cambridge, UK and made one professional appearance – in a women's contest in France. He is now working on a book about Napoleon. (p18–19)

Andy Martin's illustrative work is now on the move and increasingly features his self-scored soundscapes. (p120)

Jonathan Meades Writer of and performer in twenty-five TV films, *The Times* restaurant columnist since 1986, author of five books, currently two-thirds of the way through a new novel called *Digging For Himmler.* (p78–79)

Miles Murray Sorrell (Fuel) design group have a history of creating unique publications – their magazines were started in 1991, a book *Pure Fuel* in 1996 and a forthcoming book, *Fuel 3000,* will be published in September 2000.

Andrew Mueller writes about various things for *The Sunday Times*, *The Independent*, *The Guardian*, *The Face* and *Time Out*. His first book, *Rock & Hard Places*, was published by Virgin in 1999. (p45–47)

Shannan Peckham has written widely on nineteenth- and twentieth-century cultural politics. He is a fellow of St Peter's College, Oxford. (p64–69, 126–127, 150–153)

Martin Pesch Freelance writer living in Frankfurt, Germany. He regularly contributes to *Frieze*, *Spex*, *Kunstforum*, *Frankfurter Rundschau* and *die tageszeitung.* (p135)

Martin Plimmer Writer, broadcaster and one half of The Men Who Know. He is writing a book about household angst and has never masturbated in his life. (p140–141)

Rick Poynor writes about design, media and the visual arts for many British and international publications. His latest book, *Design Without Boundaries: Visual Communication in Transition*, is a collection of his journalism and criticism. (p26–27)

Andrew Preston writes about television for *Night & Day*, the *Mail on Sunday*'s magazine. He was mentioned in the 1984 edition of *Wisden.* (p104–105)

Richard Preston is features editor of *The Daily Telegraph* and was previously deputy editor of the *Independent* magazine. He has collaborated widely with Fuel and wrote *Pure Fuel*. (p116–119, 154–159)

Christopher Robbins is an investigative journalist and has written several novels including *Air America*. (p56–59)

David Robson is a middle-aged newspaper journalist. Having found www.olivetree.org he feels that other internet searches are superfluous. (p32)

David Roper was once described by a national newspaper critic as 'saucy' but has survived that to run one of the UK's leading radio and TV production companies, Heavy Entertainment. (p100–103)

Alix Sharkey writes about fashion, media, social trends and pop culture for *The Guardian, The Observer, The Independent, The Evening Standard* and various European and American publications. (p24–25)

Mark Sinker Cultural critic and historian, specialising in music and film. He is currently finishing *The Electric Storm*, a critical history of music and technology over the last century. (p38–39)

Chris Symes Film producer, having previously run the European division of LA-based Propaganda Films, he now has a small film company called LMI Pictures. (p110–111)

Chi-Haru Watabe Japanese freelance design journalist. Contributor for design magazines: *Creative Review, FRAME, Studio Voice, Designer's Workshop,* and *AXIS*. (p114–115)

Monty Whitebloom has directed music videos and commercials and is currently in film development with Fox Searchlight with *2gether4ever.* (p86–89)

Catherine Wilson Writer and interviewer on the *Telegraph* magazine. She went to St Martin's School of Art where she developed a debilitating shoe fetish. Her work has also appeared in *Vogue*, *The Guardian* and *The Observer.* (p136–139)

John Windsor Freelance art market writer, is a regular contributor to *The Observer, The Financial Times* and *The Independent.* (p40–44)

Gaby Wood works at *The Observer*. Her book, *The Smallest of All Persons* is published by Profile Books. (p128–131)

Is her career ruined by Joanna? Can she still become a mother?

THOSE ARE THE QUESTIONS EVERYONE NOW ASKS. Claire Miller, the 32-year old manicurist, who now suffers from nail injuries as a result of Joannas vicious assault, fears she may have to give up a very successful career as a manicurist. "Who would trust their nails to a manicurist with an ugly nail, I wouldn't", says Miller's attorney Wally McDeal of the lawfirm Suit & Case. As if this misfortune wasn't enough for Ms Miller, she fears she might also lose the baby she may be carrying. "I really would lik
to have a child so my boyfriend and I have made love every mornin
we first met two
There was a goo

COUNTRY-ROCK STAR JOANNA ATTACKS PREGNANT WOMAN.

Joanna denied entry to downtown club – starts terror

IS ONLY BEGINNING OF

The Luxury of Dirt TERROR?

EXCLUSIVE

by KEITH REINHARD

Polish-born country-rock star Joanna Zychowicz, known as Joanna, who instantly reached number one on the world's country-rock charts with her catchy hit *"Dirty Country Girl"* last summer, has since had a remarkable career. Her new CD "The Luxury of Dirt" has been climbing the charts rapidly. But everything seems to be falling into pieces. IT'S REAL has the full story. Wednesday night as Joanna was trying to enter the down town club The Twitty Twit, she was denied entry. "She wasn't properly dressed, she was wearing dirty clothes", the bouncer Mikey Bündefeldt explains. According to witnesses who for obvious reasons would remain anonymous, Joanna argued that dirt really has beco luxury in this shiny, flashy w the name of her new CD " Luxury of Dirt", indicates she w serious about it. Joanna the raised her right hand as if she wa about to hit the bouncer who the professionally avoided the assau which caused Joanna to fall. In h fall she violently grabbed anothe woman who was queuing for the club which caused them both to fall. The poor, innocent woman, who may also be pregnant, had to seek medical advice the following morning, a spokesman from the lawfirm Suit & Case told IT'S REAL.

WITNESS' PICTURE

After attacking the innocent woman, a desperate Joanna leaves the crime scene accompanied by her boyfriend Rick.

Number 105 in a series of Diesel "How to…" guides to successful living. For more information: call Diesel U.K. 0171-8332255 www.diesel.com

This advertisement is pure fiction. The characters, names, incidents, dialogue and plot are used fictitiously. Any resemblance to actual persons or companies is purely coincidential.

DIESEL
FOR SUCCESSFUL LIVING
DIESEL
o one is going
to talk dirty to me'
says victim
bouncer Mikey.
Inside report: by BOB SCARPELLI
"Joanna laughed and said her dirty jeans were a luxury, but I've been working the door for 5 years and noone is going to talk dirty to me", Mikey Bündefeldt, the bouncer at the club The Twitty Twit says and you know he's honest about it. "When you've been in this business for 5 years you know the business. If somebody raises their right hand you don't wait around for the first hit – you take action!", Mikey continues, and with his 95 kilos of pure muscles there is no reason to believe he's not capable of taking care of even tougher assaults than Joanna's brutal attack.
FULL STORY: Page 5
Get the full
story in your own
free copy of It's Real!
At your local Diesel dealer
or at www.diesel.com
IT'S REAL

Millions of brides have been shipped all over the world since time immemorial, but it took the internet to bring us 'eHusbands.com – the world's first mail order husband agency'. Amazing, isn't it, that no woman has been able to sit down and order a husband before now? Especially given that women are romantic, soulful little creatures, whose dearest wish is to find a mate and settle down. All women really want to do is get married; they're famous for it. As eHusbands points out: 'Who knows better what it is like to long for that special someone each lonely night than a woman?' That's why it took a woman – God bless her – to create the site.

Each month, eHusbands chooses a Man of the Month: 'a man that we think will make an ideal husband'. Anybody's ideal husband, because women all want the same thing: stability, kids, and a bunch of pink carnations. George (eHusband SA 234) is 53 and looks like a TV evangelist. He describes himself in terms that would obviously appeal to the doe-eyed sex. 'I love soft, intimate moments,' he writes, 'candle light, gentle music, looking deep into one another's eyes, sipping wine, and talking about each other's joys and dreams.' At last a man that doesn't prefer a beer, watching football and playing with his Black & Decker. Lost and lonely-hearted women will gasp. George enjoys 'giving the woman I love very special gifts – jewelry and lace lingerie are my favorites.' Not only can you order George by computer, he appears to have been designed by one as well.

You can preview some of the many eHusbands in the 'gallery' at the site. Here you will find men with a GSOH, such as José: 'I like writing music, singing, eating at McDonald's – just kidding, I like Arby's better.' Or like wild 'n' wacky Guy, who says 'I am a smart and funny kind of guy. I think I was Indiana Jones in my past life except I hate snakes.' A sense of humour like this is important to ensure a marriage endures beyond the initial passion. And it's well-known that women love to laugh at a man's jokes.

Some of these men are looking for a woman 'that likes to live life on the edge of her seat' – as long as she ventures no further. Others are struggling feminists: 'I love a woman that is not offended to go in the kitchen and cook a great meal that we can enjoy by a romantic fire. I will even help!' This from the only British male in the gallery (watch him, though – he lists 'soccer' as a hobby).

Given only a line to describe himself, Alan plumps for 'lovable, understanding and a non-smoker'. The three most important things about him. Robert describes himself in just one word: conservative. Robert has beautifully blow-dried hair forming a corona effect round his head. His huge shades give him that 'on the run' look. And, in fact, he lists his hobby as 'long drives in the country'. These men have been sadly passed over in the marriage stakes. And they just want to be loved. Who better to do it than a trusting little woman, one hand on her Magimix, the other on her lace panties?

There's a man for every woman at eHusbands. But as the organisation specialises in shipping husbands from abroad for consumption in the USA, British women will just have to run out and buy *Bridget Jones: The Edge of Reason* for now. If you are a man, you can send in your details free and soon have lovelorn American babes conversing with you in private chatrooms. If all goes well, eHusbands offers a complete immigration service to the US. And it's affordable. 'After all, love shouldn't cost you your life savings. (You're going to need it for that little family you will be starting soon hehehe).' That GSOH again, it's such a bonus. It's strange, really, that women don't surf the net night after night the way men do. Suppose they'd rather be cooking up intimate little dinners in the kitchen. Bless.

Susan Irvine

http://www.barefooters.org

Ever felt the overwhelming urge to cast off the shackles of your socks and shoes and stroll down Oxford Street with your feet as naked as nature intended? Ever felt that your right to walk barefoot into McDonald's or your local shopping mall is being thwarted by authoritarian strictures, or the hostility of an uncomprehending public? Probably not. But if the answer to either of these questions is 'Yes', then the website of The Dirty Sole Society is for you.

Forget the poor, the hungry, the dispossessed, The Dirty Sole Society exists to defend the right of everyone, as 'a lifestyle choice', to walk barefoot, not only in the privacy of their own home or on the beach, but on the street, in restaurants, shopping malls – just about everywhere.

This is not a right, you may think, that has great need of special pleading. But The Dirty Sole Society thinks otherwise. Their website offers a stirring mission statement about promoting 'barefoot acceptance worldwide' and 'regaining the freedom our parents and grandparents had to go barefoot anywhere', as well as providing 'a friendly forum' to 'share experiences, thoughts, feelings and tips' on bare feet, and provide a 'support group' for members, 'encouraging and helping one another to get along in a shod world'. (No, not that friendly. Browsers with more carnal interests are politely referred to another site, alt.sex.fetish.feet; frustratingly, my server wouldn't connect me.)

I chanced on The Dirty Sole Society through a link from another site, '11:11 Solara' (www.nvisible.com), a new age movement that claims to see cosmic portents in the recurrence of the numbers 11:11, notably on digital clocks. 'At first, it seems like a mere coincidence,' reads the introduction to the site. 'It must be my coffee break time.' Then it becomes uncanny: 'I started up my car at exactly 11:11'. Finally, it is undeniable. 'All my clocks froze at 11:11.' Something very strange is, indeed, happening.

Whatever it is, it can't be as strange as Solara herself – a winsome-looking brunette from Montana who contends that the number 11:11 carries 'a unique resonance which affects and activates you on deep cellular levels' and provides 'a reminder of your true purpose here on earth'. What does this have to do with taking off your shoes and socks? As one correspondent to The Dirty Sole Society movingly testifies, 'For some of us the soul is resident in the sole, and yearns ceaselessly for light and air and self-expression. Our feet are our very selves.'

A piquant mixture of the heroic and the laughable, the bizarre and the downright pathetic, the site is to be commended for its attempts to mine every last ounce of meaning and interest out of its subject matter.

There are protracted essays on the legal and medical ramifications of walking barefoot ('It is not against the law to go barefoot into any kind of establishment including restaurants'). A 'barefoot gallery' features compelling pictures of people courageously flouting convention by walking barefoot into a McDonald's on Hume highway, 100km south-west of Sydney, and entering a K Mart at Deep Water Plaza, Woy Woy – wherever that is. And there are helpful suggestions about the pleasures to be had running 'black feet contests' and – rather desperately – 'just some fun times' by going barefoot. In all honesty, as 'fun' this appears to rate somewhere below tooth decay or wearing a colostomy bag.

'Bill', e-mailing from somewhere in America, reports that after 'finally getting the nerve' to visit his local mall barefoot, he had 'no encounters with anyone', and that while the 'well kept ceramic tile' appeared clean, his feet were black by the time he left. 'But since it had just rained and there were puddles all over outside, most of the dirt had been washed off by the time we got to the car.'

Can't wait to try it yourself? The site includes a helpful network of international contacts, including an account of a barefooters' convention in Paris, which sheepishly admits that 'not many people showed up'. But it's worth persevering. As the site says, 'It's nicest to go barefoot with others who are barefoot, knowing they are feeling the same things as you are...' That's grit, tar, broken glass, spent chewing gum...

Mick Brown

This is strictly for the hardcore only, those for whom bigger is better. I propose calling us the 'Twenty-Foot Club'. I am referring to those surfers who don't even bother to get out of bed when it's a mere ten and demand full-on 20-foot waves as their absolute minimum.

www.xsurfseries.com is pornography for wave-starved surf-fiends. And yet I have qualms. There are shots here of the 1999 Quiksilver Eddie Aikau contest (for which 20-foot waves are a minimum requirement) at Waimea Bay, Hawaii. Sceptical e-mails from the North Shore at the time raised doubts about the validity of the waves. Now I see why: they are a marginal 20, definitely borderline.

Quiksilver more or less had to let the event go on this year after the scandal of 1998, when, with genuine 30-foot-plus boomers in the offing (I jest not: I was there, although keeping a safe distance), the contest was called on, then off, when the event's director put discretion before valour.

Michael Ho: Glory Tube

The slogan of the contest, 'Eddie Would Go' – ie Eddie (the legendary Eddie Aikau, who died in a heroic rescue attempt at sea) would paddle out, no matter how big the waves – had to be downsized to: 'Eddie Would Go, Providing It Was Safe', which somehow lacked the ring of the original. That was the day, Big Wednesday, the last Wednesday of January 1998, when lifeguards switched from Baywatch to Big Brother and physically prevented surfers from going out. For the first time, surfing was outlawed at Waimea. It was a kind of blasphemy.

Unfortunately, because this site is sponsor-driven, you're only going to get the good news, so you have to read between the lines. Another of the darker aspects of the noble art that this site doesn't spell out is the intense rivalry, almost a state of war, between Hawaii and the West Coast. Click on the Mavericks contest. Here you find some classic waves at Half Moon Bay near San Francisco. The key question is: which is bigger – Waimea or Mavericks?

For decades, Waimea had the title of Biggest Big-Wave Spot all to itself. It was the Holy of Holies. Then its supremacy was challenged by tow-in surfing, which opened up some new sites (eg: Jaws, on Maui) hitherto too big for surfers even to dream of. But that was OK, that was like a separate category of off-shore breaks that required unusual technology. Waimea's reputation remained intact.

Until Mavericks made its name. And it was all Foo's fault. Mark Foo, veteran of 30-foot wipeouts at Waimea, had to drown there, in mere 15-footers, one Christmas Eve a few years ago. Since when, Mavericks has never looked back. In the El Niño year, it won out in terms of the sheer quantity of big doughnuts, although Waimea still had the undisputed Biggest Day. (Ironically, the K2 award for Biggest Wave of that winter went to Taylor Knox at Todos Los Santos – click on Reef Big Wave).

Comparing this year's La Nina smokers, I would still give Waimea a slight edge. But look at all the gear the West Coast winter surfers have to wear – thick rubber hoods, booties, a total body sheath, the works. Whereas the North Shore guys are still in their shorts. In my view, if you're going to drown, drown warm.

By way of comparison, I consulted the semi-live surfcam for Fistral, Newquay (on surfline. com), which is looking huge and heavy – if you happen to be around six inches tall. The quest goes on.

Andy Martin

http://www.missingkids.org

http://www.missingkids.org

The children displayed in the gallery of missingkids.org have been severed from their own stories. Represented by a passport image and a cursory set of facts, they have become part of a single homogenous group, The Lost. They have been lured away from the mythic security of family life by some kind of bogeyman, a contemporary Pied Piper. Now they float free from the particularities of their existence in the place beyond the door in the mountain. America's National Center for Missing and Exploited Children (NCMEC) urges you to help retrieve these boys and girls by dialling 1-800-THE LOST.

Put this way, the NCMEC's mission is uncontroversial – plucking kids from the Pied

Piper's clutches and placing them back in the bosom of their families – but it takes very little probing for this vision to fall apart. Tucked away in mute information files are clues that suggest that the enemy without is more often the enemy within. Family abductions and runaways make up the larger proportion of these children. These lost boys and girls have more in common with Peter Pan's gang than the Pied Piper's drug-duped following. In the nastier and now largely unexplored parts of J.M. Barrie's story we are told that the Lost Boys fell from their prams – a clear hint at abuse – and that Wendy and her brothers follow Peter only as an indirect consequence of their own father's rage. As Barrie acknowledged, the lost are most likely to have been propelled or to have fled. Returning to missingkids.org, it takes little elaboration upon the labels of these children to arrive at the bleak realisation that, lost or found, for the most part their lives are in tatters.

While missingkids.org strives to detach The Lost from their messy histories, members.tripod.com/~nfishel acts as a forum for individual tales of loss and is dense with particular narratives. The site was established by parents who have lost their children to a 'nomadic Bible-based cult' known, amongst other names, as The Roberts Group. At its centre is a set of open letters sent to the Brothers and Sisters of the cult by their families. Reading through these letters, it becomes apparent that there is a degree of common ground between cult members and their relatives in the maintenance of this site. In spite of their professed disapproval, parents of the Brethren romanticise the aims and spirit of the cult and, although they have forsaken all ties with their families, cult members clearly anticipate and respond to these letters.

I was particularly struck by two aspects of this site: first, the hyperbolic descriptions of the qualities and achievements of the runaways, and second, that all cult members came from families of practising Christians. I came away with two pieces of advice that parents of the Brothers and Sisters might not endorse. The first is pretty standard: don't expect too much of your children, you will only encourage them to disappoint. The second might be more objectionable in the religious climate of North America: to prevent your children becoming Brethren, you might be wise to refrain from Christianity altogether.

I know it is obscene of me to judge families that are facing tragedy, but by expanding upon what it means to be lost, the parents of The Roberts Group have made themselves vulnerable, a vindication perhaps of the NCMEC's policy to keep the category of The Lost entirely unexplored.

Emily King

http://www.SiddharthasIntent.org

When his debut feature film was selected for the 1999 Cannes Festival Critics' Fortnight, 39-year-old Bhutanese director Khyentse Norbu suddenly found himself tipped as the year's hot new directorial talent. Asked to list his favourite films, he included Oliver Stone's *Natural Born Killers*. Norbu has a flat in Notting Hill Gate, travels the world virtually non-stop, wears Armani shirts, and his award-winning *The Cup*, the first full-length Tibetan language film, is all about the link between religion, tradition and... football.

Despite all this, Tibetan Buddhists regard him as the living reincarnation of a Buddhist saint. He rises at 4am each morning to begin his five-hour session of prayer and meditation, studied philosophy from the age of 9 until he was 23, and was personally tutored by the Dalai Lama. Under the ecumenical title of Dzongsar Jamyang Khyentse Rinpoche, and through his Siddhartha's Intent International organisation, he is responsible for the education and welfare of hundreds of monks in monasteries and colleges in Tibet, India and Bhutan, and has Western lay students all over Europe, Australia, Asia and the USA.

Not surprisingly, perhaps, his web pages are a little less formal and more sophisticated than many of those devoted to Buddhist topics and teachers. An elegantly designed and informative site, its overview page gives potted biographies of both DJK (as he is known to his students) and his principal teacher, the late scholar saint Dilgo Khyentse Rinpoche. This information is contextualised by a brief, jargon-free history of the Khyentse lineage, and a sort of mission statement: 'According to Buddhism, the nature of enlightenment is to uncover mind's inherent wakefulness, and the outcome of such enlightenment is to strive for the relative happiness and ultimate enlightenment of all sentient life.'

Seekers looking to get involved will find pages with teaching schedules, photos and information on retreat centres in India, Bhutan, Germany, France, Canada (luxurious, and set in beautiful mountainous countryside) and Australia (isolated, in the outback). Meanwhile, those who prefer to check things out from a distance can read teachings and interviews online, or order audio tapes of recent teachings given by DJK and other invited lamas at his centres. These range from highly esoteric expositions of Madhyamika philosophy, to simple, down-to-earth advice on meditation and its role in everyday secular life.

But perhaps the classiest touch is the site's Gentle Voice newsletter, which features interviews with DJK and his close colleague, Chokling Rinpoche (one of the stars of his film, incidentally). Here the subtle profundities of the Tibetan Buddhist vajrayana path are explained clearly in an interview with DJK, while the hopes and fears of his heart-broken students are held up to scrutiny in an amusing but apparently genuine lonely hearts column called 'Dateless and Desperate'. Sample ad:

'Long-time student, ex-coffee addict, multi-talented, tree-house dweller with a penchant for woollen gowns and dancing a Scottish jig, requires a mechanically minded, male dharma student who will help service her taxi, follow her on her wanderings and keep her warm all year round. Please contact the editor referring to the code name: Eyrie.'

The site's only real inadequacy is that it doesn't belong to the Dharma Ring network of Buddhist web pages, which would allow links to related pages. Still, as spiritual websites go, this one is easy on the eye, well constructed and with enough effortless wit to make it attractive to both practitioners and non-aligned surfers alike.

Alix Sharkey

http://www.cacophony.org

Organised chaos might be an oxymoron but that's what the Cacophony Society seems to offer. 'Cacophony is everywhere' announces the society's homepage in lurid letters above an outline of America that has been filled like a gas tank with molten images of a clown's face, a huge model dinosaur and a guy fondling an alligator. Don't be deterred by this limp graphic greeting because the verbal side shows a lot more imagination. This random gathering of eccentrics is out to discover experiences 'beyond the pale of mainstream society'. A multiple-choice manifesto explains they are square pegs in non-Euclidean holes, holy fools of casual enlightenment, the monkey virus in the big top, and oh yes, Dada clowns (the Cacophonists do love their clowns) rewiring the neural circuits of the nation. The day when some soulless ad agency swipes the society's perfect come-hither slogan – 'You may already be a member!' – can't be far away.

The Cacophony Society really does appear to have branches everywhere. The main site is a jumping off point to Chicago, Detroit, Cleveland, St Louis, Brooklyn, Atlanta and Seattle, among others. Some of these sites have a disconcertingly parish newsletter air. In August, for instance, you could have enjoyed lemonade and a game of 'mondo' croquet with the Portland chapter. Not much prospect of cognitive dissonance there, one feels. No, for heavy-duty weirdness we must turn, as always, to Los Angeles, where the 'Reverend' Al Ridenour leads a gang of performance artists, psycho-terrorists and assorted stop-at-nothing party animals up the path of excess to the throbbing palace of Extreme Transgression.

The LA site is persuasively written and genuinely funny. A three-step guide to Cacophony culminates in a Socratic exchange between Reason and Unreason. 'In our events,' says Unreason, 'we celebrate bad films, cheesy lounge music, crank cults, redneck gun shows, morticians, naive artists, transvestites – anything that could accelerate the decay of traditional aesthetics... We've befriended the barbarians on the other side of the fence, and we've given them the bolt cutters.' They've organised field trips to mortuaries, public sewers, folk art sites and cryogenic labs, staged UFO encounters and an Easter egg hunt at an abandoned Nazi camp, and put on a parade of junk-encrusted 'art cars'. They've shopped on Rodeo Drive covered in mud and dropped by city hall dressed as circus humour personnel (OK, clowns). In the archive you can see the Museum of Mental Decay, a Santa orgy (something about the jovial gift-bringer brings out Americans' Inner Subversive) and Reverend Al in a big red nose.

There's a listing for international Cacophony groups on the main site, but all three are in Canada – a simmering stew, it often seems, of every variety of radical dissent. In a forum on one of the American sites, I came across a lone English voice calling for help in setting up a Brighton branch. Not a bad place to start, but no takers so far. As for the expertly synchronised American Cacophonists, can a corporate sponsorship offer be far behind? Happily, these guerrilla clowns are just about crazy enough to say shove it.

Rick Poynor

Feel like rebelling against senseless consumerism? Here's a safer alternative than resorting to automatic weapons.

Simply get yourself into the thick of it and bring along a camera – video,

SLR, Lomo (if you're really trendy), disposable (if you're planning to get into a fight with that security guard) – and join in the fun by 'shooting back' at the surveillance technology that records our every move while we shop.

You won't be alone. According to its no-nonsense website, National Accountability Day is an annual happening coordinated by UK and Canadian groups – an 'international coalition including artists, scientists, engineers and scholars'. The design is simple: Times Roman, a couple of pics, FAQs and a manifesto, with no effort wasted on prettifying a simple and convincing message. For entertainment value though, there's a twisted line in logic and some amusing lingo.

'The Bigs' are the shopkeepers. 'Totalitarian Establishments' are those that 'wish to know everything about everyone yet reveal nothing about themselves', i.e., they take pics of you but don't appreciate it when you whip out a camera. So, 'what's good for the goose is good for the gangster'. Worried about what to shoot? The site provides guidelines, i.e., 'models will quickly be dispatched, usually wearing blue uniforms'. And, as we're so often told that video surveillance is provided for our own protection, the logic of NAD suggests that shooting back is a way of returning that kindness.

NAD may be a coalition of black-clad anarchists or simply a chat-group of armchair activists, but kooks or geeks, they've got a point. Do you like the idea of being filmed in a changing room? It happens, and guess where those images end up? Surprise, surprise, broadcast over the web. The question, must freedom be sacrificed for the sake of security, isn't new – the site quotes Thomas Jefferson on that one – but as always, technology has upped the stakes. Does one store in London's Oxford Street really need 250 cameras?

Judging by the success of such initiatives as Adbuster's Buy Nothing Day, and the grass-roots response to the World Trade Organisation's Seattle conference, there's evidence that previously apolitical individuals are not only getting fed up with Big Brother, they're getting clued-up. The inquiring gaze of the corporate camera treats every shopper as a potential thief. It is that sort of intrusion to which National Accountability Day acts as an effective counterweight.

Liz Farrelly

http://www.flashmountain.com/index.html

I don't know about you, but I've always had my doubts about this whole tit-flashing business. In fact, I'd even go so far as to say that, aside from one thoroughly amusing afternoon at university watching a beautiful fellow student lift her jumper and startle the life out of a roomful of computer nerds, I haven't a good word to say for it.

I'm certainly not against breasts *per se*, nor the idea of them being revealed to total strangers at unexpected times in unexpected places. And yet, a bit like adoring raw tomatoes but being unable to stand the sight of tomato soup, I find myself strangely unmoved by a site wholly dedicated to what we might call acts of Opportunistic Female Nudity. Why so? After all, those wacky guys at flash-mountain.com have gone to no little trouble to beg, steal or borrow (it doesn't indicate which) a wide selection of photos of ordinary young American women lifting their tops in all manner of public places – principally, and hence the site's name, in front of the tourist record camera on the Splash Mountain log flume ride at Disneyland, Florida.

Nice, all-American girls, daringly flashing their dollies at Disneyland (and, more subversive still, interrupting the free running of capitalism by ruining the souvenir photo-op for the other families in the car)? Surely not. It couldn't be allowed. Well, yes it could, and in such numbers, too, it makes you wonder if there isn't a sign at the top of the ride asking for at least one volunteer per car to do their duty and free the puppies for Old Uncle Walt.

Doubt it somehow. To most Americans – and, on some level I would guess, the boys behind the site – such acts are deeply, pleasantly, erotically profane. We're not just talking about any old log flume ride here but Disney's finest – Disney: all seeing, all knowing, Great White Father, keeper of the flame, guardian of the American dream. To trespass like this under Pluto's very nose. . . why, if there is an act more mad and dangerous and fuck-off horny than this that the average trainee teacher can commit without fear of prison, then hell, Bud, I don't know it.

Uhuh. That's right. If you like to feel smug and superior to certain types of Americans and the tragic extent of their capacity for real rebellion, then this is the site for you. Now excuse me. I'm off to destabilise the economy by buying my paper with an old Irish five pence. Wicked.

Harry Crabbe (Jnr)

Come the Day of Judgment, when we are all called to account, it will matter not a widow's mite how we answer the question: 'What were you doing when you heard that George Harrison had been stabbed?' And whatever your response to the inquiry: 'What did you think when you heard that Ian Wright had been awarded the MBE?', it will not have you weighed in the balance and found wanting.

But happy will be the man or woman who can put hand on heart and say this: 'At the moment of the second coming, when the Redeemer returned to earth to save me from my misery and lead me back from my waywardness, when He walked through the Golden Gate in Jerusalem's Eastern Wall, I was there. Well, virtually. I was logged on to Messiahcam, on www.olivetree.org. Verily I was.' Such are the nurturing arms of the net: amidst all the hubbub is a still, small voice. There, devoted and eternal in its vigilance, is Messiahcam. It does not blink nor turn away. In its eye, neither mote nor beam.

No righteous soul can doubt that the evils of the internet, its compulsions and repulsions, are many and various: they cause family breakdown and mental decay and physical decrepitude. They play havoc with personal hygiene. And we know their source: the weaknesses of the fallen. For it is as easy for a web-addict to enter the kingdom of heaven as for a rich man to pass through the eye of a camel. Brothers and sisters, the temptation that led man from paradise to perdition was an apple. Thankfully, it may now be the good offices of www.olivetree.org that help to get us back into the Garden.

This is not a site you visit then turn away from. For who can know the moment at which the Messiah will choose to return? And who can risk being elsewhere when that moment arrives? Messiahcam is a vigil interrupted at your peril. 'And where were you when He ascended the Mount of Olives?' you will be asked. 'Absent surfing? Perusing the sci-fi catalogue on amazon.com?'

One can only pray not. And so, abandon hype, abandon soap, all ye who enter here. For, like regular numbers in the Lottery, this site – once chosen – can never safely be quit. Who created this site? Who deemed it meet? One Christine Darg appears to be its earthly mother and Salinas, California its not surprising manger. But for its true source, you must look back down the millennia. In an interview with a California newspaper, Darg said: 'In the Great Commission, Jesus commanded His followers to go into the world to preach the Gospel, and part of the world has become the World Wide Web.'

The sweet chariot is out there, my brethren and sistren; only foolish eyes would be turned elsewhere when it comes for to carry you home.

David Robson

A MONTANA MASTERPIECE

In Xanadu did Kubla Khan
A stately pleasure-dome decree…

Thus the divine Samuel T in the summer of 1798. Sedated with opium, in a lonely farmhouse on Exmoor, he slept for three hours and had a vision – half dream, half poem – 'in which all the images rose up before him as things, with a parallel production of the correspondent expressions, without any sensation or consciousness of effort.' As soon as he woke up, he grabbed a pen, ink and paper, and wrote 'Kubla Khan'.

Lucky Sam. Meanwhile I, rum-crazed and pixel-blitzed in El Periquito, my cabaret-brothel home in Havana, wander the measureless caverns of the internet, seeking some shred of style, beauty or intelligence… What a desolate search. All my time seems to be spent riding a mouse down a purple corridor upholstered with booby-trapped buttons. Touch one by chance and it flings you into a warehouse filled with repulsive three-piece suites. Touch another and you are in some ghastly person's front room, inspecting their panoply of bad taste memorabilia. There are nasty salesmen everywhere, smelling of beefburgers and deodorant. True, there are naked girls and boys, but you can't touch them, they're no good, for they are conjuror's illusions, made up of flickering bitstreams. I don't like this place or the creeps who hang out in it. Everything is crass, tantalising and cynical.

Opium nightmares have nothing on it.

And so I think of the great Samuel T. In Xanadu, he saw the perfect website – 'in which all the images rose up before him as things... without any sensation or consciousness of effort'. This is the beauty of a supercharged imagination. Samuel T didn't need the internet.

Such were my gloomy thoughts until a friend pointed me to the Montana Testicle Festival – www.testyfesty.com... Ah, that sudden breath of transatlantic air, like a window flung open on a stormy night! Now I've been there, seen the website, bought the T shirt – and come home with the crazed light of the convert in my eyes.

Go there, friend. View its glittering albums of revelry. Bask in its roast-meat colour scheme. Read its touching history – how Rod Lincoln, a school superintendent, bought the Rock Creek Lodge Motel (known as 'the Snake Pit') and set up his testicle festival there in 1982. Marvel at its Garden of Eden nudity, its culinary wonders ('beer-marinated, secret recipe breaded, deep-fried bull testicles'), its simple, good-hearted daftness.

Browse through the festival programme – Body Painting! New for 1998! Come drink your favorite beverages and take the stage... paint your favorite body parts with safe, non-toxic, fluorescent paints! As always at the Testy Festy... clothing is optional! Bullshit Bingo. At this event, a Bull Calf is led around a HUGE bingo grid... The square in which the cow shits... is the winner! The person that bought that square for $5... WINS $100. 'Bite the Ball' Motorcycle Ride. Motorcycle riders or their passenger attempt to bite a hanging testicle as they ride by. Check out the Testy Festy Store, a true shrine of the grotesque ... And don't miss the Guest Book, where punters like Robert quip 'It takes a lot of balls to put on a programme such as yours', while Dave, torn between the confessional and the billboard, announces, 'My friends and I have been having our own testicle festivals for years now and we're going international. I'm organizing the first ever Internet Testicle Festival for 2000.' (Thanks, Dave, see you there.) A man called Rodney is so inspired, he promises to spend the rest of his life in Montana, like some latter-day Desert Father. Another, of more patriotic bent, finds it 'fabulous that we are now concentrating on men's nuts instead of women's breasts, at this Festival anyway. Ain't America great?!' Well, yes, Ron, I suppose it is.

There should be more websites like this one. It's a work of perverse genius. I think even Samuel T would have enjoyed it.

Medlar Lucan

FESTIVAL
SHOW ME
NUTS
ROCK
LODGE

http://www.vix.com/menmag

Why is being a man so difficult? What has made men need so much protection, counselling, so many self-help books to cope with their masculinity? The scent of fear coming off this website is tangible: a fear, as well as resentment, even anger, at the way men's lives have been complicated, marginalised and threatened by the consolidation of women's role in the workplace. Women have moved out of the home into the office, and, most dangerous of all, have won the battle of the campuses in America. Feminist-inspired politics have turned American college life into a reign of terror, subjecting male and female students to a near-hysterical policing of the ordinary motions of the human body. While leading feminists have shown themselves to be louder and more clever than their opponents, champions of masculinism – the word is clumsy, but then so, perhaps, is the idea – have found themselves facing an ironic crisis: no one wants to be seen as a fast car-driving, jockstrap-sniffing Neanderthal, not even Jeremy Clarkson (an inexplicably, if briefly, popular television presenter in the UK), and so those leaders in the various 'men's movements' which sprang up across the Western world over the past twenty years developed a new way of talking about masculinity. The fact that they were talking was a feat in itself, but the language they use, for all its invective towards feminists (as seen in this website), is saturated with a ghastly touchy-feelyness which would

once have been derided as pathetically girly. Now that feminist politics has so influenced the mainstream, now that male supremacy in the city is no longer unquestioned, men who yearn to find out what it is to be male seek refuge outside the city walls, away from the offices where the slightest masculine relapse is watched by the beady eye of political correctness. They yearn to become wild men. Deep in the forested hills of Minnesota, Yorkshire or Bavaria, men of all ages get together around fires and open up to each other. Not sexually, although I'm sure this would just be considered an intimate bonding moment, but rather emotionally, since, as we know, men just can't deal with their emotions.

Back home, alone in their bedrooms or late-night offices, they log on to MenWeb, a site listing the latest seminars, books, articles, and events about 'male issues': these include 'feeling and expressing our unique energy' or 'healing sexual shame' by attending workshops in which they practise drumming, poetry, story-telling, and psychodrama, 'as a way of stalking and connecting to the wild man'. Some of these writers, conference leaders, therapists – whatever – are very angry men. They talk about 'gender justice', the righting of the bad reputations men now supposedly have just for being men, or 'mythopoesis', the discovery of the poetry of masculinity as evidenced by the examination of ancient warrior myths and sagas. Employing a vocabulary lodged somewhere between *Planet of the Apes* and *Star Trek*, they write about holding 'Talking Sticks in Councils', and make themselves into 'Promise Keepers'. The sad truth is that for all the talking, all the promises to be good and kind, the level of debate, the sharpness of argument just isn't there. The amusing thing is that while feminists have taken so much trouble to de-sanctify conventional notions of womanhood, these men strive so hard to define masculinity by constructing a curiously quaint notion of it.

Mark Irving

http://www.wcs.net.au/~bessie/sunhill/index.htm

This series of pages, run from Australia, is named The Jasmine Alley, after the troubled Jasmine Allen Estate, as reluctantly policed by the bobbies of Sunhill, in the long-running UK TV cop serial *The Bill*. On the site are photos of characters, links to official episode guides and other credit details of interest to fans, accessed by phrases related to routine storylines: ID parade, evidence locker, community liaison... But the real content is this: erotic male-on-male fantasies, written by female fans, about characters from *The Bill* (so expect to see adult content warnings when you find the site).

Review: fan literature and the slash aesthetic

'I've often had fantasies,' wrote rock critic and radical feminist Ellen Willis in her scathing 1973 review of *Deep Throat*, 'about making my own porn epic for a female audience, a movie that would go beyond gymnastics to explore the psychological and sensual nuances of sex; incidentally, the few porn movies I've seen that deal with these aspects of the erotic were made by gay men.' Willis, an unrepentant Sixties libertarian and lucid exponent of sexual liberation, would by the Eighties be battling to rescue feminism from panicked anti-porn repressiveness. Meanwhile, an invisible army of butter-wouldn't-melt housewives had seized the initiative, quilting together a multi-authored 'porn epic for a female audience' from the most unlikely material, in the form of beautiful fanzines, typed and pencilled, then Xeroxed and exchanged at – of all places – Seventies *Star Trek* conventions.

The zines explored (to quote Willis further) 'the power of sexual tension and suspense; the conflict of need and guilt, attraction and fear; the texture of skin; the minutiae of gesture and touch and facial expression that can create an intense erotic ambience with a minimum of action', as might occur in physical encounters between Captain Kirk and Mr Spock, coded K/S (later just slash), so as to evade suspicion.

So, home-made homoerotica was born, blooming from mass-media characters denied this key dimension precisely by their mainstream origin, existing on the sly edge of legality. Discovering such infractions, the entertainment industry at first ignored them, to avoid public embarrassment. Once slash was on-line, the industry was trapped: admitting awareness left it hostage to huge potential copyright payouts, since incidental but recognisable non-sex elements from slash storylines had inevitably, if coincidentally, been replicated in official episodes.

Though it predated the net, this phenomenon also very much prefigured it. Hence, today, a domesticated explosion of slash websites and links, from cheesy Seventies icons *Starsky and Hutch* (the duo, legend says, that inspired the very first erotic fan-lit) to end-of-century fantasy cult classics – *The X-Files, Buffy, Xena* – by way of *Ally McBeal, The A-Team, Babylon 5, Blake's 7, Due South, Dukes Of Hazzard, E.R., Friends, Hercules, Homicide, MacGyver, Man From U.N.C.L.E., M*A*S*H, Miami Vice, Mighty Morphing Power Rangers, SeaQuest DSV, Spenser for Hire, Twin Peaks...*

There is no great subversion in discovering a polymorphous subtext in *Xena*, scripted since its outset with a knowing eye to a Queer audience, with net feedback a key resource. But viewer-writers worldwide are becoming ever more daring, rising to challenges ever more implausible – projecting dreams and desires, for example, on to the most solidly, stolidly quotidian English drama: not just *Queer As Folk, The Professionals* or *Dr Who*, but *Dalziel and Pascoe, Inspector Morse* and – courtesy of Bessie in Australia – *The Bill.*

Mark Sinker

Flight Of The Elephant $75,000

It's bad art, all right, but is it Bad enough? Connoisseurs of the genre are sticklers for the fine points of Badness, as a cruise of the inverted art-snobbery at badart.com will reveal.

Take the 'masterbad' painting, 'The Ugliest Duckling'. Please. The self-styled Bad Art connoisseur Vito Salvatore has posted it with a tag of $250,000, having bought it for an undisclosed few bucks at the Antique Co-op in Hyannis Centre. The square brushstrokes, he sniffs, knowledgeably, are meant to convey a 'blocky pointillism'. It is, in his opinion, 'a noble effort... which wonderfully and utterly fails... The duck looks plucked, bloody and scabbing as it staggers about looking for a merciful chef to cut off its head. Stunningly and gorgeously hideous!' You get the idea. Clever-clogs Salvatore is looking for that pinch of pretentiousness, that hint of hubris, that can elevate mere incompetence to the toe-curling heights of Bad Art. Nudge, nudge, chortle. But he admits: 'You always know you have a winner when a look of disgust descends over the thrift store owner's face'. So anyone can become a connoisseur of Bad Art, then? Perhaps there's hope for those of us who simply know what we like. Or don't like.

As for the astronomic price tag. Well, there's always a chance that what seems truly Bad may turn out to be truly Good. And Bad Art does have an art historical track record.

http://www.badart.com

SKULL LADY PAYS A
SCONCERTING VISIT TO JOHN IN THE
OSPITAL WHILE FLAME-PEOPLE
BRING
CHOCOLATES!

It was Philip Guston who coined the term, back in the early seventies, when he threw away his reputation as an Abstract Expressionist by painting the crude, cartoonish 'Painting, Smoking, Eating' – a self-portrait of a fat, unshaven slob in bed with a plateful of sandwiches, puffing a cigarette. It was an expression of self-loathing. The period, the time of Watergate and defeat in Vietnam, Guston had joined protest marches, then retreated to the cosiness of his studio to fiddle with colour harmonies. His conscience is now salved and his Bad Art is bankable.

Charles Saatchi – not a likely patron of ugly ducklings – stumbled across the Bad Art trail when he visited the Californian 'trash painter' Jim Shaw's show of naff thrift store art at New York's Metro Pictures gallery in 1991. Another visitor to the show was Goldsmith's graduate Martin Maloney, now Britain's best known Bad Artist, whose splodgy, seemingly amateurish figure paintings found their way into Saatchi's *Sensation* show in 1997. Maloney is bankable, too.

The catch is that, no matter how gloriously naff your thrift-store finds may be, it takes an artist with a college degree to break into big-ticket Bad Art.

But there's no shortage of aspirants at badart.com. Do you detect deliberate intent in the dribbles and daubs, the tasteless nudity and religious motifs? Then you probably have on screen not a thrift-store find but the work of a self-taught Bad Artist trying to earn a quick buck. These are not amateurs trying to be Good, but amateurs trying to be Bad. Their failures are not glorious, but pathetic. But as failures equally complete.

Meet self-styled Bad Artist Eddie Breen, aged 43, from Massachusetts, who claims to have sold his 'Christ's Flesh', oil on canvas, for $500. He explains: 'A lot of stuff happened over the years. Now I mumble a lot and paint sort of scary or weird paintings. People who know me keep their distance when I drink coffee, because sometimes I throw it. There's a big hole in my house where my kitchen should be. I eat cold food out of a can.'

Breen is plainly confused. He is muddling his genres. No, Eddie, it's not Bad Art that you're trying to imitate, but Outsider Art, the stuff discovered by the French artist Jean Dubuffet. You don't have to be an art college graduate to do Outsider Art – just mad, locked up, or both. And there's a catch to Outsider Art, too. As soon as you go commercial, buyers start complaining that you're not loony enough. So watch it.

Any good art hidden among the Bad? Well, there are two thrift pictures I liked, an unpriced 'Maid Spraying Kids on Second Floor With Hose' and a discovery by Salvatore of two heads, artist unknown. But for the $15,000 he is asking, he can stuff it.

Salvatore gets complaints. A correspondent accused him of displaying pictures that obey the rules of classical art. Chastened, Salvatore has promised to showcase in future 'only the REALLY, REALLY, REALLY bad stuff, and not desperately purchase a painting that sucks only a little'.

John Windsor

It is scarcely any wonder that David Bowie has taken up the cyberspace cause with such crusading fervour. He has, after all, spent the entirety of the 1990s charging wildly, even dementedly, between media – designing wallpaper here, bashing out a few paintings there – in what has been a fairly transparent attempt to distract attention from the ever-impending 20th anniversary of the release of the last album he made that any sane person would rather listen to than eat.

Bowie loves the internet, feels at home there, and it is no wonder at all. In the history of human cultural endeavour, only pop music before it has offered such latitude to the congenital chancer: both arenas value style over content, form over meaning. And just as Bowie's recording career has been a (remarkably successful) exercise in elevating a few vaguely entertaining lightweight boogie records to the status of art by dressing himself up as a succession of sideshow prizes and pretending to be a martian, so his much-vaunted ISP, BowieNet.com, is a common-or-garden fanzine-cum-souvenir stand posing, risibly, as a beacon on the path to the future.

If BowieNet.com is nothing more or less than another fan site, it does at least have the virtue of being created and/or sanctioned by Bowie's biggest fan – himself. Bowie's bottomless fascination with all things Bowie is best demonstrated by the choice of links offered by BowieNet: where other personal homepages might direct the reader to sites dealing with, say, favourite television programmes, artists, seafood recipes or especially interesting recent developments in igloo engineering, BowieNet offers links to 250 – count 'em – more sites concerning David Bowie. The image conjured is not attractive: a glassy-eyed Duke gazing fixedly into his screen into the small hours, running interminable searches on himself on ever more obscure engines, emitting increasingly intermittent yelps of triumph as he pins down another chronically mis-spelt, black-and-white, two-page cyber-homage emanating from a dung-powered webserver in Gabon.

BowieNet also offers a chance to help Bowie meet his doubtless gargantuan telephone bills, offering for sale an assortment of pointless junk quaintly described as 'Accessories' and 'Collectibles'. In the former category are the inevitable BowieNet mouse-pad and sheet music for his records – possibly best thought of as an extended illustration in how not to do it. In the latter are such ephemera as posters, lithographs and programmes, some of them autographed – proving beyond doubt what a boon the net is going to be for no end of has-beens with well-stocked attics and a marker pen to hand.

Inevitably, BowieNet also boasts a chat room which, in fairness, offers two richly rewarding avenues of entertainment. One is to try convincing everyone else in there that you actually are David Bowie, popping in for a quick mingle with the fans; for added effect, and/or if you're especially bored, ask a similarly-minded friend to log on at the same time and do the same thing. The other is to start by asking the assembled obsessives 'What did he ever do, anyway, other than dressing up in Bacofoil and rewriting *Tiger Feet* by Mud with lots of nonsense about spaceships and transvestites?', wait for a fight to erupt, and then leave.

Andrew Mueller

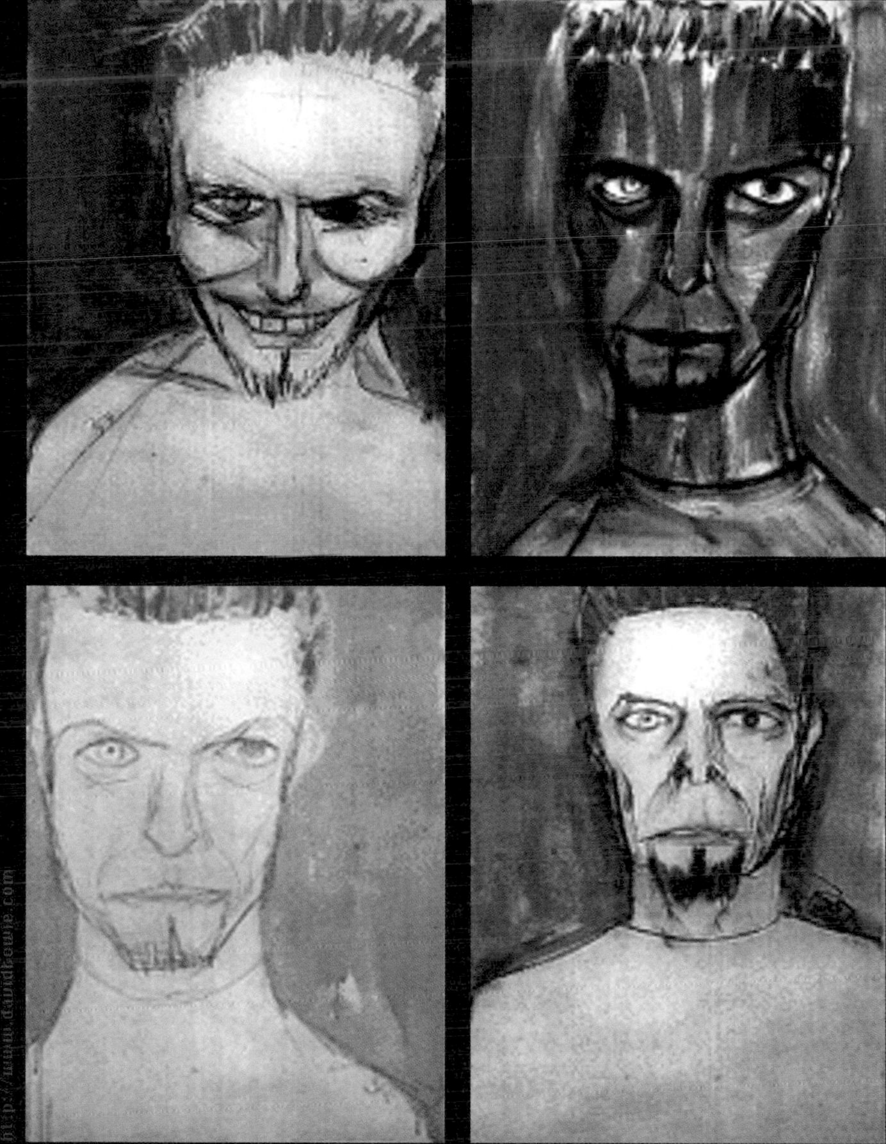
http://www.davidbowie.com

Saul Bass is, at first sight, an unlikely hero of the world wide web. He is, for a start, dead. However, on this British site created by fan and designer Brendan Dawes and co-fanatic, Victor Helwani, Saul Bass is revealed (again) as not only the great graphic genre stylist in cinema, but also a uniquely translatable artist.

In web terms, why does the Bass approach work so well? Well, let's say that the sans-serif, cool, Ariel-heavy world of a myriad sites, the hit or missness of HTML text, hasn't given up the ghost just yet, but Bass online manages to make it feel very, very dated: very mid-to-late Nineties. For if design works in this frustrating medium it has to be strong, bold and simple; if typography as information can triumph amid the many 'Buy' buttons and shopping basket logos it has to be instantly memorable. Bass's visual legacy – those gorgeous meshy angles from *North By Northwest*, the striking simplicity and blood rich red of *The Bird Man of Alcatraz* or *West Side Story* film posters – work wonderfully, even on my dirty old laptop computer.

Dawes uses Flash, a software technology that, to date, has not always been the most joyous of web experiences. Here Dawes succeeds with this tricky plug-in to create a small environment with sound, icons and moving images which is part homage, part gallery exhibit, part portal link to other web resources. The site has at all times, however, the feel of Saul Bass – other than, curiously, a downloadable and editable shower sequence link from *Psycho*, should one feel the need to improve on Alfred Hitchcock's montage skills. Dawes uses the famous Dead Guy cut-out from Otto Preminger's *Anatomy Of A Murder* as the concept for the navigation of his gallery. His launch page image-checks *The Man With the Golden Arm*, the filmography slides in the *North By Northwest* grids, and the illustrations of Bass's continuing influence is wryly titled, and graphically influenced by *Advise and Consent*. Sound is nicely employed as part of the interface in the prints section. Roll over a thumbnail and an audio clip spits from the Duke Ellington soundtrack to *Anatomy Of A Murder.*

So Bass, fuelled perhaps by his late work with Martin Scorsese, shows every sign of Darwinian resilience: his style, as Richard Dawkins might say, is a meme. At best his work combined a 1920s Soviet poster quality with a broody postwar American spirit of spatial vastness and psychological disruption. For that graphical communism we now read, click and buy e-commerce; for the vastness and disruption there are now the dislocating revolutions coming about in business, communication and organisation simply because of the web.

Saul Bass feels right for these e-times. He might not be the future of web design, but his iconic vision will surely still be around when some very tasty web designs from the Nineties have fallen off the Server in that Great .Com in the Sky.

Robin Hunt

http://www.zeldman.com/ ad.html

Here's the thing about advertising: after years in which industry cheeses have bumped up fees by selling the idea of their creative minds as Artists with a capital A, the creative minds have bought into the myth wholesale. And if there's one thing that an Artist hates, it's being ignored. Oh, the pain when an idea bites the dust: the hissy fits over the Chardonnay, the pins stuck in the client dolls, the beaten-and-starved egos. I worked my fingers to the bone for these people: I was up all lunchtime, and what appreciation do I get?

So hooray for Jeffrey Zeldman, whose Advertising Graveyard allows thwarted creatives the opportunity to have their work seen despite the pitiful lack of imagination client-side. The premise, certainly, is a fun one, particularly in our media-savvy age: punters can log on and see the ads that never made it, chortle over puns, howl at on-the-edge-humour, gasp with admiration. And it all starts well – an ad by Zeldman himself for a microbrewery that in the event never opened: 'One of our authentic double bock beers and you'll feel like you're in Germany,' reads the copy, beside a gleeful picture of a stereotypical man enjoying a long cool glass of something. 'A few more and you'll feel like invading Poland.'

Good one: Zeldman obviously has one of those stains-on-carpet senses of humour that gets the pressure groups up in arms. This is rapidly followed by another fine example from a campaign written in his days at Grey Entertainment for a TV special starring the surviving Beatles: 'They said it would take 3 more bullets'. Even John Lennon would have laughed at that.

Except. The problem with a submit-your-own website is this: it takes a rare personality – a minor Royal, perhaps, or a morning TV presenter – to deliberately volunteer to show off their pratfalls in public. With the very occasional noble exception, the dead ads on this site are ones that their creators feel dented pride in: the ones that were killed because the client was too stupid, or too timid, or too hide-bound to accept them. Here is not the place to find examples of Really, Really Bad Ads; the puerile jokes that came out of too much time locked in the lavatory; the moment when someone failed to spot their own double entendre or leapt over the boundary that distinguishes black humour from bad taste. There are some good gags here, and plenty of examples of individual brightness, but in the end, how long do you want to spend listening to teenagers show off?

The Advertising Graveyard is, at least briefly, a laugh, and is no doubt brilliant for buffing individuals' CVs, but in the end what you come away with is an overwhelming sense that if these people were paid a bit less, they might be doing something a bit more useful.

Serena Mackesy

http://www.stuart-tiros.com

U
CONNECTICUT
U

http://www.stuart-tiros.com

Metaidentity: a psychological definition of one's perception of other people's perception of oneself.

'Welcome to my life!' The presupposition of the Stuart Tiros experience – the family snapshots, the lists of favourite films (*Animal House*, *Close Encounters*) and music (Nirvana, Queen) – is that someone, somewhere is going to be interested. There's no justification, no interpretation – merely the Stuart Tiros-ness of Stuart Tiros III, a serial-numbered, gypsy-haired downhome boy from Gainesville, Florida, with two earrings.

It is as if he believes that the effort alone of having scanned his family album into cyber-space gives meaning to the banality. Yet there's a deadpan quality to his photocaptions you could source to Raymond Carver via J.D. Salinger and Oprah Winfrey: 'Me and Rebecca playing with friends in the kitchen. My parents still have that wallpaper.' 'This was taken the night I left here to attend the University of Connecticut. I still don't know why I just had to leave that night.' 'My ex-wife Chloe and I, just before our divorce.'

The self-dramatisation is the product of a therapy culture in which to be you is an end in itself. 'Stuart Tiros III' is a logical manifestation of the confessional memoir, kiss-and-tell world.
Its darker side is exposed in the 'Private' file, a love letter to his current partner. Here, the naked Tiros is presented in the manner of a reader's husband, a model from a medical text-book, or a tortured police suspect: tanned, hairy, pot-bellied and unspectacularly endowed, a sexualised counterpoint to innocent shots of the toddler Tiros naked in the backyard.
Isolated in his own white cyberspace, Stuart Tiros, consciously or not, has invented himself as a media persona. There is no reason why we should be any less interested in him than in David Beckham: 'Stuart Tiros III' sounds like a Warhol multiple and, like a Warhol character, he is up for his fifteen minutes of fame – extended to infinity on the net.

But there remains the essential existential dilemma: would Stuart Tiros exist without me as a spectator? Underneath the self-affirming normality, the reassuring nuclear family, the suburban existence, are hints of what might be, or what might have been. The brief window of escape to high school, now reduced to a few beers after work; the undescribed relationships, the untold grief of separation and divorce; the – ohmigod – alienation of it all.

In the light of what we do not know, Stuart Tiros's grinning face assumes a rictus of desperate self-assertion, an attempt to convince himself, and me, of his existence. Stuart, I'm still not sure.

Philip Hoare

http://shoko.calarts.edu/~alex

I have just met my first net millionaire. Cool, clever, laidback and pushy. Californian, in other words. I asked him what it was all about. After a lot of babble about equity splits, AOL paper, debt streams, burnrate and incubation he gave in and explained. 'It is,' he said, the glint in his look hardening, 'all about eyeballs.' I said 'Uh-huh', but plainly did not understand.

He explained that here's a business that, for the first time in the history of capitalism, is valued on the basis of potential growth rather than present or historic profit and loss performance. 'You gotta,' he went on, 'get twelve and a half million eyeballs.' Discounting entirely the possibiity that 'eyeball' is a Palo Alto neologism for an obscure electronic component, a witch doctor's algorithm or an arcane protocol, you are left with the anatomical interpretation. Not counting the one-eyed, twelve and a half million eyeballs means six million two hundred and fifty thousand people.

That, he enlarged, is what you need to have a viable e-business. You just gotta hook these eyeballs, lock in a third party investor and sell out before anyone realises what is happening, or, in Old English, 'that they are being had'.

The steam age metaphor he used to romanticise the process was: imagine America in the 1850s and you are galloping west. You stick a stake in the ground every time you reach the geographical equivalent of twelve and a half million eyeballs, mark out your territory and gallop on. You keep on sticking stakes in the ground until you run out of North American landmass. In our calendar terms, that's about four or five years of Wild West business practices before it all gets formal and h-e-a-v-y.

At the moment, eyeballs are not attracted to the net any more than poets find e-mail a useful expressive medium. E-mail may yet find its laureates, but so far it seems a peremptory medium best suited to very basic messages, not much more useful, poetically speaking, than using a long-handled axe to carve letters in a tree. Visually, the net is similarly hobbled. Look up some of the world's best known graphic designers – say Milton Glaser in New York or Pentagram in London – and you can see that they are struggling to come to terms with the aesthetic limitations of the net.

But at least their struggle has some classical, tragic dignity. None of those noble attributes clings to shoko.calarts.edu/alex. Here, I gather, is some sort of attempt to recognise that the net is a new medium requiring new disciplines. It's an on-line version of, I think, ironic Post Modern sampling: random images from webcams are overlaid for the delight of the viewer. My Power Mac 7300/166 may be a bit creaky, but it took a long, long time to have the screen filled. A cheerful warning came-up: 'cultural recycling takes a minute or two'. You bet. Seemed longer. And it was not worth it: my bookmarked webcam at Geneva's Cointrin airport is much, much more fun. There were moments when this site accidently achieved a visual density close to Rothko, but my eyeballs prefer what you can find in The Tate. Links took me to Hank, the world's most photogenic feline. I was, sad to say, the two hundred and seventy one thousand one hundred and eighteenth pair of eyeballs to log-in here.

Ah me, what eyes hath love put in my head/Which have no correspondence with true sight? The thing about the web is: the medium is the medium. It can't do art: that's old media, old eyeballs. Poetry is what gets left out in the translation. Take out the electronics and all you have left is the boredom. The question remains, how do you get eyeballs if you cannot get art? If you worry about this sort of thing, you'll never get rich.

Stephen Bayley

http://www.bcpl.net/~rfrankli/hatedir.htm

http://www.bcpl.net/~rfrankli/hatedir.htm

The Hate Directory helps hate-mongers – ranging from the merely disturbed to the criminally insane – to find their very own niche of negativity. The directory lists groups and individuals that in the opinion of its compiler, 'Advocate violence against, separation from, defamation of, deception about, or hostility towards others based upon race, religion, ethnicity, gender or sexual orientation.' The Hate Directory promises something for everybody.

Hundreds and hundreds of sites are listed with helpful pointers to each one's orientation. After all, a man who hates Jews might not necessarily want to waste his time hating lesbians, although many followers seem to be equal opportunity haters. Hate surfers can log on to the Hate Mongers Hangout, or the Nazi Café, and interact with the Internet Racism Discussion Board – guaranteed to get the blood pressure surging and create an evil mood.

Racists are legion – sometimes religiously inspired, but often just fired up with good ol' secular bigotry. A host of so-called Aryan American Ku Klux Klan backwoodsmen are listed: 'Check out the Aryan Women Egg Site – people with superior genes make a super white baby!' There are Honky Hackers (displaying an unusual trace of humour) who no doubt regularly check the Racetraitor Home Page: 'Treason to whiteness is loyalty to humanity.' Huh? Hold on, are these guys white or black? Who are we supposed to hate here? There's even a children's chapter of the white racist cult World Church of the Creator. And for those who have burned out on the old Black/White thing there's Fear of a Third World Planet (in case anyone forgets to hate the yellow people).

Religion generates its own white hot hatred. There are Satanic anti-Christians, Christian anti-Semites, people who hate Muslems, and Muslems who hate Zionists. Sites like Jew-Rats and Jew Watch are listed alongside Why Christians Suck. Holocaust denial is rife, although there are those who think it didn't go far enough, as represented by Better than Auchwitz (sic – spelling is not among the hate-mongers' strong points; along with syntax, logic or any other tool of the rational world).

Gender hatred has a committed following. There are sites for the Society for Cutting Up Men (SCUM), the Man Hating Dyke Club Militia, and Misogyny Unlimited. According to the twisted sister that posts All Men Must Die, the site receives 120,000 hits a year. 'That's 10,000 people on average a month who see me as a man-hating potential mass murderer/ serial killer maniac,' she boasts. 'Cool huh?' And don't get this crowd started on gays. God Hates Fags (religion and homophobia overlap here) is one of a multitude of anti-gay sites, although Queer Power helps to redress the balance by advocating the subnormal nature of heterosexuals.

In some instances, where it is no longer possible to log on to listed sites, hatred seems to have burnt itself out like certain advanced cases of leprosy. Other sites are offered for sale, presumably aimed at those who have hatred in their hearts but are too lazy or too stupid to start the ball rolling on their own, and need to buy some hatefully nurtured Bad Will. But the world of hate is a cosier club than the members of the disparate groups might wish, for the vocabulary of hatred is severely limited. Although all the groups naturally loathe one another, there is a similarity in the mind-numbing monotony of their messages. Black or white, Christian or Jew, gay or straight, while the object of hatred changes, the sites fundamentally remain the same.

Stray from the demented, repetitive ranting of the groups into the loony landscape of the individual and the vision becomes even more tedious in its uniformity. Teenage Americans challenge the surfer to enter their worlds. It does not, of course, take much courage to enter a website, but for those prone to melancholy it is advisable to have on hand a bottle of aspirin, a shaker of dry martinis, and a prescription for Prozac. These geeks seem to think their worlds are weird and threatening, when actually they are predictable and dull. Hatred might stir the emotions, but it seems to smother the imagination.

What to do? No code governs the outpourings of these hatemongers, and it is unlikely that any law could ever be devised that would work effectively. There is no voice to challenge, no forum to debunk, no channel for effective criticism, no opportunity to point and laugh. Even if sanity could be e-mailed, it is unlikely it would be downloaded.

The Jewish Anti-Defamation League offers a Hate Filter, a software product designed to act as gatekeeper to protect children. It's something, but the ADL is oddly defensive and careful to make clear that it does not seek to censor or close down the sites, which shelter behind bogus claims to free speech. The ADL has accepted an inescapable truth – bottom-feeding weirdos on the net are a fact of life. I say, if you can't beat these turkeys, join them. Hate the bastards!

Christopher Robbins

http://www.kt.rim.or.jp/~khaosan

Welcome to Khaosan homepage. To Corpse Museums in Thailand.
To the Crime Museum. To the Surgery Museum. To Miserable Affairs in Thailand.
To beaming children on a school trip. Now, please, go to a chat room and chatter about what you have seen.

http://www.maskon.com/marti/index.html

The Female Mask Homepage opens self-consciously, with a quotation from Oscar Wilde: 'Man is least himself when he talks in his own person. Give him a mask and he will tell you the truth.' The epigraph gestures to a philosophical context within which the viewer might read the creators' penchant for latex masks. If you're after the philosophical, or for that matter the weird, prepare to be disappointed. While the site includes a summary of masks as featured in film, in the media and in fiction, it doesn't live up to the grand claims of Wilde's pronouncement. There is something homespun – even quaint – about maskon.com. The style of the site is that of a chatty and homely cross-dresser cutting and pasting with a mug of tea around the kitchen table. The conversation is about masks, but it might just as well be about the relative quality of tea-cosies.

The Mask Homepage is the creation of two cross-dressers, Kerry and Martin. In maskon.com, the 'one-stop resource of female latex masks on the internet', Kerry introduces himself as 'a straight, male cross-dresser who loves to make and wear Lycra costumes along with heels, wigs, and latex masks'. We learn that Kerry is 38, lives in Seattle and attends science fiction conventions. There is nothing weird about Kerry, except, that is, when you remember that s/he has a fetish for masks. But then s/he's into the solid, earthy latex variety.

For all the philosophising and the self-conscious nod to Wilde, there is no depth to maskon.com. We are introduced to the creations of Paul Barrell-Brown, which can be purchased for $225. There's a chatty, rambling description of Martin and Kerry's Tokyo adventure with Yuki and members of the Japan Pantyhose Fetish Club, together with some innocuous chat in the inevitable chat-room. The surfer begins to suspect that nothing much is being concealed. The theory goes that by donning a mask an individual loses his inhibitions and so is able to externalise his fantasies. This is a theme that dominates popular culture. Think of the repressed doctor in Stanley Kubrick's *Eyes Wide Shut* (1999) who attends a masked orgy, or the timid bank clerk Stanley Ipkiss, who uncovers his dynamic alter ego in Charles Russell's *The Mask* (1994) so that the schmuck finally gets to boogie with the beautiful heroine. The mask in both cases is liberating, although the freedom it brings has its price. Strip away the latex masks from the models in maskon.com and what do you find? Thirtysomething middle management science fiction buffs from North America. This revelation brings its own terrors, certainly, but it hardly stops the heart beating.

On the one hand, the mask functions as protection. On the other hand, it is the vehicle of violence, and the anonymity of the mask bequeaths

power: from tribal witchdoctors to Batman, the stockinged face of a terrorist, and the ghoulish Halloween mask. If the masks do disturb in maskon.com, it's because of their passivity and inexpressiveness and because they singularly fail to perform the function that we expect masks to perform. The female mask gallery offers a selection of mostly indistinguishable masks that resemble the giant pumpkin-heads of monsters in 1970s sci-fi thrillers, over-pumped rubber mannequins, or the blanched faces of unusually bloated Noh actors. There is finally something nostalgic, even retro, about a site that promotes masks on the internet for anonymous surfers who are masked by the very technology that brings them the masks. We can assume the mask of anybody and everybody in cyberspace. What need, then, for a latex tea-cosy?

Shannan Peckham

http://www.maskon.com/marti/index.html

http://www.mayhem.net/Crime. serial1.html

There are some questions you can't help pondering in times of tedium or insomnia. What would be my replies were I ever asked to do the *Guardian* questionnaire? What was the name of the third Charlie's Angel, after Kelly and Sabrina? Does my bum look big in this? And which serial killer would I least like to share a flat with?

I've worked out the first three: witty but meaningful ones; Jill (later replaced by Kris); and, probably, in unwise trousers and unflattering light. In search of an answer to the fourth, I paid a visit to mayhem.net, home to a chart – yes, a *chart* – of serial killers, mass murderers, killer cults and rampage killers. (Slogan: 'They tried it! They liked it! They did it again!') It's like the Top 40, only not as grisly.

Top of the, ahem, hit parade is a fellow worse than all five of Westlife put together, if you can imagine such a thing. Pedro Lopez, undisputed Monster Of The Andes, who 'tallied an impressive 300 slayings' during the 1970s. His victims were spread across three South American countries and were all female. So a male flatmate would be safe unless they happened to confuse Pedro with a convincing bit of cross-dressing or anger him by suggesting someone else was Monster Of The Andes. Besides, you'd only get the pleasure of nomadic Pedro's company for a short period before he moved out – no doubt forgetting to pay his share of the bills, but leaving some nice knife-sharpeners as compensation.

In like a bullet (so sue me) at number two comes Henry Lee Lucas, who gained fame not only by claiming to have killed 200-plus, but from the quasi-accurate biopic *Henry: Portrait Of A Serial Killer*. Henry often worked with an accomplice, Otis Toole. The site cheerfully dubs them 'The Tag Team from Hell'. A houseshare with Hank and Otis would be inadvisable. Henry was into necrophilia and Otis into cannibalism, which led to all sorts of petty fridge disputes ('Did you lightly sautée my girlfriend in ghee?' 'But you hadn't written your name on it'). Equally unsuitable co-habitors include three-figures killer Pee Wee Gaskins (could you honestly take phone messages for someone called Pee Wee?); a Ukrainian called The Terminator who shot 52 innocents and during his trial claimed to be a 'bio-robot' (he'd be constantly watching Arnie vids, meaning you'd miss your favourite soap); and 38-scoring South African, Moses Sithole (same problem as Pee Wee, with added risk of rude spelling mistakes).

Still, the one I'd least like to share a flat with is Japanese karma-cult leader Shoko Asahara, the God Of Poison heavily suspected of masterminding the Tokyo subway gassings. This 'blind, portly guru' recruited scientists to manufacture him truth serum and nuclear weapons, and sold vials of his blood to followers at five grand a throw, while telling them to 'renounce materialism'. Best of all, he repeatedly dozed off during his trial, asked witnesses to levitate and float across the courtroom towards him, and clutched his own head for hours on end, 'to stop it from exploding'. The guy is plain weird. Wonder what his *Guardian* questionnaire answers would be...

Michael Hogan

Japanese karma-cult leader Shoko Asahara

http://www.webexcel.ndirect.co.uk/aichair/index.htm

Be it drinking champagne from a woman's sweaty stiletto or simply the fine curve of Victorian furniture, we each have our unique fixation. For Llwyd, creator of the 'Hair Today, Gone Tomorrow' website, the obsession is women – bald women. Specifically, actresses who have gone bald for their art. 'Many actresses have appeared in films without their hair,'

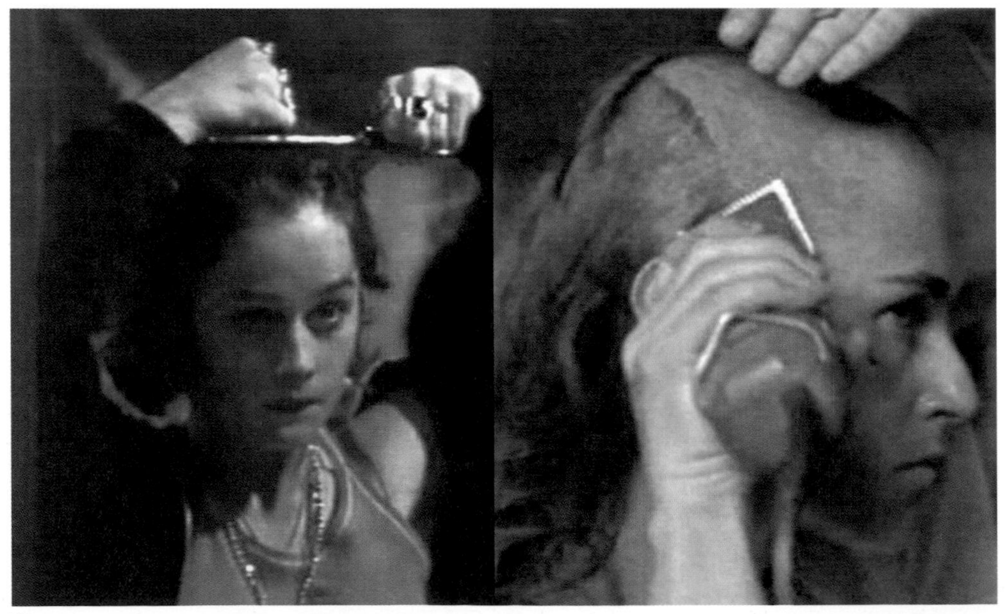

he writes. 'Usually this has been achieved with the assistance of the make-up artist and a bald cap. But sometimes for the part an actress undergoes a transformation that goes beyond make-up.'

Note the distinction: the integrity of an actress making what Llwyd calls 'the ultimate sacrifice' – losing her hair, as opposed to using mere cosmetic trickery. Clearly, Llwyd is suffering from some intense psycho-sexual hang-up. Probably to do with his mother. So his cause is fascinating. 'Why do they do it? I'd like to think it was for the art but mostly the films have been exploitational or the baldness/shaving a stunt. Those particularly vulnerable... seem to be young actresses attempting to make a mark or those whose career is on the slide,' he opines.

Confused he may be, but the research is pretty thorough. His Hair Today & Gone Tomorrow site takes us from *Star Trek: The Movie* to *GI Jane*, picking up untold, obscure telemovies along the way. And yet, there's something missing here (and I don't mean hair). Llwyd can't figure out what makes a bald actress so striking. Like a proletarian art critic, he just knows what he likes.

But as Mr Spock would have it, bald women are the final frontier. They exist so rarely in real life – a clichéd lesbian here, a Mo Mowlam there – that every snapshot would appear to have some profound significance. As human beings we are revulsed/attracted by deviations or deformations. A man without legs? You notice the stump. A woman without hair? You see the scalp.

This applies tenfold to beautiful women. Actresses and models are our universal objects of desire, a global shorthand for excitement and adventure. They sell us shampoos and holidays, beers and cars. To shear them of their femininity is to make a statement, of empowerment or disempowerment. Think of Ripley in *Aliens*, whose hair got progressively shorter the tougher she became. Contrast this with the Jewish women of *Schindler's List* – shivering, bald and naked as they await a possible final shower. These images let us in on a secret: underneath the hair, there is something more real – be it vulnerability or strength – than simple titillation.

Oliver Horton

http://utenti.tripod.it/berenice

I've always thought there was something slightly unsavoury about really long hair. All that cherishing and washing and brushing and eking out of long dead fibres: it's not a million miles from taxidermy, is it? What's more, it's a fairly reliable rule of thumb that anyone who grows their hair beyond the base of their shoulder blades without a good reason – say, a lucrative modelling contract with a shampoo manufacturer – is weird.

Pure bloody-minded prejudice, of course, which is where the internet comes in. So ill-informed yet forthright that you can't even get on air on your local late-night radio phone-in show? Get on the net. Thanks to The Long Hair Club, I am now confirmed in my opinion that long locks are not only unhygienic, but also just a hair's breadth away from a litany of misdemeanours ranging from incompetent spelling to chauvinism, body fascism to the total inability to construct a sentence.

As with many web journeys, it begins innocuously enough, in familiar overgrown pen-pal style. 'Hello! I'm Florindo, your friend living near Naples,' he begins, sounding like an MTV Europe VJ. 'I love hair very very very much.'

Florindo's club, Berenice's Kingdom, is open to 'every man or woman who has love and passion for long and very long hair – Fashion is an astounding fun.' To enter Berenice's Kingdom, you have to have hair at least 20 inches long – more or less middle back length. So far, so fair enough. Then it gets a little weirder.

Every member takes the title of Pageboy. Those whose hair reaches 30 inches, about waist-length, are appointed Prince. The member with the longest hair of all is the King of the club. 'Main activity in the Berenice's Kingdom is caressing hair,' Florindo explains, promising 'exciting (mixed too) contests of caressing hair reciprocally, also competitions of caresses on hair as long time as possible.' Steady on, Florindo. Suddenly, like a mumbling drunk who leans in for a wet kiss, he lurches into capital letters. 'LET RUN YOUR FINGERS THROUGH A LONG SOFT HAIR FRIENDLY!' I suppose a sexual subtext is only to be expected of a site fetishising hair, itself a potent symbol of virility; nonetheless, Florindo is getting a little too friendly for my liking.

The only good thing about talk radio is that when bores outstay their welcome, the producer can cut them off. On the net, these people roam wild. Berenice's Kingdom has not satisfied Florindo's ambitions. Point at the sketch of a (short-haired) man clasping a girl manfully in his arms and you are magicked into Florindo's other site, the Rocking Ladies Academy. 'On wedding day the bridegroom lifts his bride on the threshold of house. Then it's never happening again for all life. All women complain and are discontented. Why on earth?' Why indeed?

Beneath a photograph of himself, this time with his long hair tied neatly out of sight, Florindo di Monaco explains how his enthusiasm for twirling women in his arms led him to write a book called *I'm Gallant and Boast.* With such chivalry, who needs syntax?! 'All women are children, babes, little ones at seventy too!'

We're on dubious ground now, but I'm still unprepared for the outburst that follows. 'Many ladies complain their partners don't carry them in arms. Why? They weigh too much, a lot of ladies grows fatter and fatter, it's woman's duty keeping a teenager figure and being thin, slender, nimble for all life, how a fat woman will demand to be lifted and rocked as babe?' Charmed, Florindo, I'm sure.

Jess Cartner-Morley

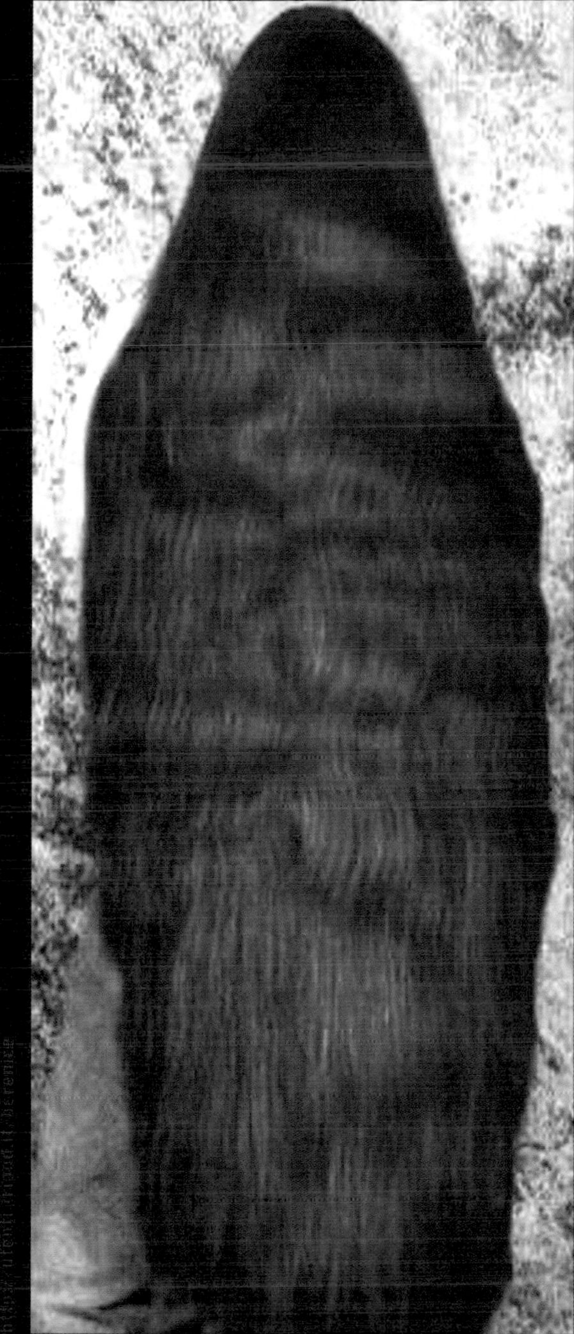

http://www.jinet.net.au/~althomp/austelo/jeff/index.html

One of the many ways in which politicians of any party are out of step with the people whom they are risibly said to 'represent' is that they still have grubby little secrets. At least they try to have: it is a problem keeping secrets when every peccadillo has a price and the press treats bumptious perjurers like Archer and Aitken as though they were mass murderers – it's Blair that drops bombs, remember.

The 'national outpouring' after the death of the Princess of Wales – Clunk-click? No – was merely confirmation of the Liverpudlianisation of Britain. Ever since Bleasdale and Brookside, and the man whose name I've forgotten who wrote *Cracker*, that city with its lovable heart on its scally sleeve has set an example in sententious self-pity, wounded sentimentality and self-righteous bullying to a willing nation: indeed it's been at it for rather longer – witness John Lennon's despicable 'Imagine'.

Shame, Liverpool tells us, is a thing of the past. And without shame there is no need for secrets. I sometimes wonder whether the net wasn't a scouse invention. It certainly militates against covertness. It encourages the propagation of grubby little secrets which, once upon a time, propriety and self-regard would have caused us to keep buried. But now they are to be shared – more than shared, shouted unto the world.

I was a bit bemused three or so years ago when I sold a house to a couple in their early sixties who said that they were going to build on an extra room for Mr ----'s collection. Collection of what, I asked. Collection of Dinky Toys, he told me – proudly. The best one can say is that he was, inter alia, a garagiste and so had some sort of... Hell, that's no excuse. Sixty and playing with Dinky Toys. He probably has his own website. A generation or so ago he'd have kept his toys with his copies of *Knave* in a trunk in the loft, guiltily. Now, along with every other geek, he has turned exhibitionist.

Make that deflected exhibitionist. It isn't exactly flashers that the net turns us into. Rather it allows the sad fuck within to come to the surface: it's the inner anorak who eagerly outs himself (it is, invariably, a him). Search down Dinky Toys at dinkymania.com or dinkytoy.com and you fetch up with the usual fanatic/collector/dealer types.

Anoraks is more fruitful: the-threshold.org (Anorak Offroad/ring.html) is the site of, I assume, a terminally sad loner called the Anorak Offroad Club – the people who read the UK.rec.cars 4x4 news group, a very informal group who want to drive there (sic) 4x4,s (sic) off road then drink beer. In other words, will someone, anyone, please come for a ride in my four wheel drive Lada? My current favourite, and the one I carry my Thermos and Marmite sandwiches to with the greatest respect, is www.iinet.net.au/~althomp/austelo/jeff/index.html – a strangely magical Australian page devoted to nineteen hairstyles worn by Jeff Lynne from the age of about eight to the present day.

Lynne is one of the greatest of all pop musicians. He wrote, sang, played lead, arranged and produced Idle Race, the late Move, ELO, the Travelling Wilburys, Roy Orbison, George Harrison, Del Shannon, Tom Petty, etc. He is at once an original and a virtuoso pasticheur. At its best, his work manages to sound absolutely distinctive yet simultaneously to be a synthesis of all pop's history. And this is also what he has achieved with his head. He is often to be found wearing at least four or five coiffes at the same time, summoning in a different way all of pop's history – it would be fatuous to pretend that pop is not just as much about sideburns and bostons and DAs and body perms and bobs as it is about riffs and middle eights.

Jonathan Meades

http://www.knix.net/alaskrafts

Ever since I was a kid, I have loved hats. When I was three years old, I wore my father's national service bush hat night and day. (In 1956, my father chose to do his service in Malaya, to be free of my mother, his new-born child, and to be able to relax in the sunshine playing his trumpet.) Very early on, I discovered, to my disgust, that it is not possible to sleep in a hat and still wake with it upon your head. No matter how low I pulled the peak over my eyes, when I woke in the morning the hat would always be lying there, useless, on my pillow.

Billy Childish photographed by his father in 1966

When I was seven, I bought an old fedora from the Bleakwood House jumble sale with my thruppence pocket money. I have a photograph of me, stood in my parents' back garden in worn-out slip-on plimsolls and my elder brother's hand-me-down jumper, carrying a flaming bamboo cane spear and with no front teeth, smiling out from under that glorious hat.

I begged my grandfather Lewis to find me a WW2 steel helmet from his work in the dockyard (he had been in the Home Guard during the War), but he drew a blank. After hunting around junk shops for months on end, I finally managed to track down a steel helmet in school. I swopped it off Nigel Moth during dinner break for an old radio receiver out of a Lancaster bomber.

I wore that steel helmet everywhere, walking miles and miles, my head aching under its weight, determined to absorb the power of the hat, even if my neck snapped in the process. I've given up playing war so much, but to this day, I carry on wearing hats with total abandon. To my child's mind, life is nothing but a game of dressing up and pretending. I am a pretend writer, a pretend artist and a pretend musician, but I play with all my heart. Hats transform me; they are magical and full of the power of their purpose.

People tell me that I'm an anachronism. Fine, I admit to it – I'm a dreamer and belong in a different age, a time when not to be wearing a hat was to be walking around stark naked.

But though I come from some lost generation of hat wearers who despise all trappings of modern technology, I have, nevertheless, had my old typewriter hidden at the back of the

http://www.knix.net/alaskrafts

cupboard and found it replaced by something called a 'computer keyboard', (which, my girlfriend tells me, you only need to touch, not hammer). She has also patiently explained to me about the wonders of the internet, so, looking out of the window and seeing that again it is winter, I type 'fur hats' into the machine. After following only a couple of empty leads, I arrive at Alaskrafts Fur Shack, where Steve and Kathy Fields sell not only fur hats, but hats with heads, tails and paws attached. The choice is extensive, including beavers, coyotes, silver, red, blue or white fox, lynx and wolf.

Seeing a whole dead wolf turned into a silly hat was a bit too sad for me, so I decided to investigate the rest of their site. I found 'Baby Mukluk Snow Angels'. Mukluks are boots, which are made of 'rabbit fur decorated with real beads' (as opposed to fake beads, I suppose) – the 'Snow Angels' are little Inuit dolls dressed in 'one-piece rabbit fur outfits with the ruff trimmed with Reindeer fur'. The Snow Angels then sit in the Mukluks, as if they are doll-sized sleeping bags.

Steve and Kathy sell an array of other fur-clad dolls, including Sourdough Sam: 'Sourdough is the word to describe someone who has been in Alaska a very long time'. Sam is a small bearded chap who comes equipped with his own hunting rifle. 'Sam's hand-painted porcelain face is covered with a thick curly beard and eyebrows.'

There is also an employees' photo gallery, but my favourite page of all is dedicated to Ethel, a life-sized mannequin whom the Fields keep chained up outside their store, winter and summer. Ethel is naked, bar her corkscrew wig and her 'world famous arctic fox fur bikini, hand made by Kathy'. One photograph has her wearing a customer's cycling helmet. 'Tens and tens of thousands of tourists have had their pictures taken standing next to Ethel!' I liked Alaskrafts very much, though my computer turns itself off whenever it feels like it. If I ever do decide that I really need a wolf fur hat (with head, paws and tail attached), then I won't buy it over the internet but will instead travel to Delta Junction, Alaska and buy it from Kathy and Steve Fields, face to face, then have my photograph taken standing next to Ethel in her arctic fox fur bikini.

Billy Childish

http://www.perp.com/whale

Big. Dead. Smelly. Not my favourite adjectives. Probably not anyone's. But there is something intriguing about this website dedicated to an Exploding Whale – a hint of the exotic, the surreal, the interestingly insane.

The story is simple. A 40-foot, 8-ton whale is washed up on a beach in Oregon. It is dead and rotting. The smell is atrocious. Something must be done. A genius in local government assigns the problem to the Highways Department. Another genius there decides that blowing up the whale with a half-ton of dynamite will be the quickest way to dispose of it – the idea being to shred the beast so finely that seagulls, crabs and other scavengers will clean up the mess. As it turns out... but let's pause here and interact. What do you predict will happen next? Think about it. Half a ton of dynamite in an 8-ton whale. That's a lot of whale to disperse, but it's also an enormous charge. Make a note of your prediction. Maybe draw a diagram of the blast, compare notes with a friend. Now read on. The explosion tore huge, crude lumps out of the carcass, flinging them far and wide. A storm of blood, blubber and whale meat rained down on the spectators and their cars, causing panic and destruction. The seagulls, scared off, never returned. A large section of the whale was left unexploded on the sand.

www.perp.com/whale lovingly documents this bizarre episode. There's an amusing account of it by humorist Dave Barry. There are photos. There are solemn assurances that this is no urban legend. There are letters, there's even a video – ultimate touchstone of reality!

If you have a flash enough computer, you can watch this video. The site courteously warns you that it will be expensive – 11.1 megabytes, at least one hour's download time with a 28k modem. (The alternative, RealVideo, although supposedly free, seems to involve buying software for $29.90.) I decided to go for the download. On my first attempt, at night, with all of America on the internet, the file transferred so slowly I calculated it would be 4 am before I could watch, so I gave up. I tried again the next morning: 85 minutes of downloading, ending in failure. No explanations given. I began to doubt if this thing was real, but tried once more, for luck, the next day. Slowly, the megabytes racked up: 10.3...10.5...11.1... success! Ninety minutes download time, and a tiny screen-within-my-screen played me a two-minute local TV report of the incident. I watched it again, still online. It was scratchy, low-resolution, but good. It was workmanlike. It sounded real. And yet... 'Our cameras stopped rolling after the explosion,' says the reporter. Really? How strange. And how incompetent. We hear a series of thuds and voices of alarm, we see a car with a crushed roof, but none of those flying lumps of whalemeat... It's not exactly compelling evidence. I suspect a hoax.

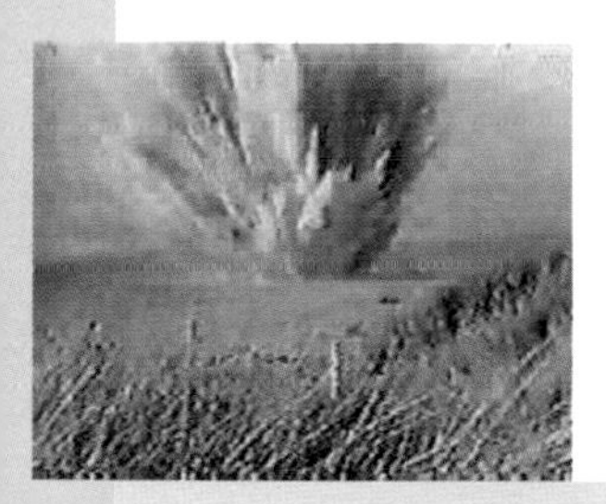

Going back through other pages on the site, I find more classic signs of a piss-take, chief among them the assertion by Dave Barry that 'I am absolutely not making this incident up'. Perhaps it doesn't matter whether it's true or not. Belief or disbelief carry no consequences. The more interesting question is why anyone should bother to construct a website on this topic in the first place.

The usual answer is that someone's making money out of it. The obvious beneficiary here is Dave Barry. The first of many links from this site is to a page on the Random House website all about Dave's books. And what a joker he turns out to be, with titles like 'Dave Barry Is From Mars and Venus', 'Dave Barry's Only Travel Guide You'll Ever Need', and so on. If it's all for his benefit, well OK – it's fun and, as advertising goes, it is at least moderately subtle and intelligent. (Dave also provides some amusing links of his own, to sites of staggering kitsch, like blond body-builder 'Fabio', with his pin-up photos and magnificently banal thoughts on 'touching', and 'remembering'; or, for real pervs, the one containing all the pictures you could ever want of deformed frogs.)

But there's more to this site than indirect advertising. It's interesting in itself. The design is crude but effective: grey parchment background, a minimum of words and pictures, no distracting messages, just a column of hot buttons down one side. The content is funny and sharp. The letters page is a beauty ('I saw your webpage URL in a magazine, and being disgusted by the title, decided to see exactly how bad it was. It was worse than I thought. This website is a disgrace to the entire Internet'). It's this weird marriage of clever presentation and pointless content that gives the site its appeal.

It's also a good story, with a classic comic structure and plenty of resonance. It gets you thinking about life, about man and the sea, dynamite and whales, and what stupid shits we can sometimes be.

But its real stature becomes evident when you follow up the links to sites like Justin Sane's Museum of the Weird, or the Looney Links Hall of Shame. In two swift clicks you are in The Dark Lair of Infinite Evil, Death Most Unnatural, or (is this better or worse?) The World of Farts and The Dog Poo Page – tacky, drivelling splurges of uselessness that give a whole new beauty to the concept of censorship. Surf that tide of idiocy for a while, and you return to the beach in Oregon with a sense of relief and, yes, oceanic well-being.

Alex Martin

http://www.wamsat.com/men

This kind of website is very common. A place to voice your ideas. A place to voice your passions. A place for everyone. A place where no one knows your real name

and no one can see the expression on your face. You can be whoever you want to be. However silly, explicit, or stupid. Freedom. Free speech. Free love. Freebird.

This is QUICKSAM's site. His hobby. His obsession. His world. He doesn't seem that interested in dialogue. I mean there's not even any chat in the chat room. I e-mail him. He doesn't e-mail me back. Perhaps it's only meant to be a monologue, with no q&a. Just a soapbox.

As I scan the illustrations I start to get the heebe geebees. I mean 'QUICKSAM' is not only dedicated to the billboarding of his obsession but he has time on his hands to be able to do so. Although the site has a sexual content, in fact the stories are explicit, the tone of the material is light and flippant. The illustrations would not seem out of place on the back of a school exercise book. They remind me of Yes and Genesis record covers. Gothic illustrations with a few flying elephants thrown in for good measure. This site is an extension of a doodle. As a starting point it contains just enough information to make it seem hollow, too much information to let your imagination loose.

Monty Whitebloom

www.wamsat.com/men

http://www.primenet.com/~novak/fleg07.html

Sometimes, ancient meets modern and ancient wins. So it is on the net. New Spam is what you don't want: it's junk mail – spin-doctored cybercrap that clogs up your virtual arteries. But Old Spam has substance and plasticity, which is why artists take it and mould it. The best of them enter Spam-carving competitions, and one of them, Dale Novak, is good enough to share his work with the rest of us. Look, enjoy... just don't eat it.

http://www.kilaita.com/joey/haha.html

The digital revolution was supposed to turn us all into models of modern efficiency, slaving away in our anonymous cubicles with machine precision. So a recent piece of research revealing that only half the e-mails sent from offices are actually work-related came as a pleasant surprise. The people fight back: after all, what are the combined forces of Silicon Valley, Bill Gates et al when compared to the desire of the average office drone to avoid work?

It is a given that any new technology will find its most popular usage in ways not intended by its inventors: just look at the way pornography has driven the popularity of video, CD-Rom and now the internet. It's a kind of moral trickle-down effect in reverse, with the low minded and trivial paving the way for worthy uses to follow.

And what more trivial use can the internet be put to than the distribution of what can best be described as 'gagmail' – e-mailed weblinks, jokes, 'humorous' lists and funny/repulsive/pornographic images (still or video) – that makes up a large proportion of this hi-tech skiving? Corporate e-mail systems are regularly crippled as workers download large image files of Bill Clinton's crotch or animals doing the funniest things sent to them by friends to brighten up a dull day. Though downloaded from the internet, many of these images, especially video clips, originate from old media. Daytime TV is a particularly rich source. Many of the clips winging their way around the world's e-mail systems originate from shows such as *Jerry Springer*. These are videoed and then typically converted to QuickTime movie files which can be e-mailed and played by most PCs. One very popular clip of a woman with extraordinary pop-eyes originated in just this way. Similarly, images from magazines or books can be scanned, saved and sent with ease.

The preparation of such files requires considerable effort, a fact that would seem to suggest that either there are a lot of people out there with too much free time on their hands or that the clown's passion for 'makin' 'em laugh' has found a new outlet, even if the longed-for sound of laughter has been replaced by a :–). Stranger still is the growth of original material devised especially for the purpose of gagmail in the hope of attaining such cult status as Bad Day, a video clip in which an enraged office worker hurls his PC to the floor in frustration, or Elephant, in which a zoo worker slips while cleaning the floor of an elephant's cage and ends up with his head rammed up the unfortunate pachyderm's backside. These clips are fast becoming the classics of a whole new genre that has grown up independent of any organised industry or movement.

One of the few gagmails that could only work on the internet can be found at www.kilaita.com /joey/haha.html. This address can be innocently e-mailed to a friend with an invitation to check it out. Type in the address and you appear to be heading for a normal website until an alert message pops up welcoming you to the site. Click on OK and another message pops up saying 'Hope you enjoy it'. Then another: 'Keep pushing OK to continue on to your surprise'. Then another: 'So, while were [sic] waiting how are you?' OK. 'Hope youre fine.' OK. 'I'm fine too thanks for asking.' OK 'But you didn't ask did you?' OK. 'You don't even care how I am do you?' OK. 'You think this page created itself dont you?' OK. You've made it mad, and this thing could be going on for some time. In fact, it keeps going for 150 alert messages. Quit doesn't work, nor do Back or Forward 'becuase as long as these little boxes keep popping up you're stuck'. OK. Not only is this thing menacing, it's also illiterate.

When, finally, it is over, you are granted access to the surprise – entrance to one Joey Kilaita's secret site containing a couple of lame *Star Wars* jokes and a link to his homepage, the Dungeon of DestruXion, which is still under construction. Should you wish to return to the secret site having perused any of these tempting offers, the whole alert nightmare starts over.

Once you've suffered, the immediate incentive is to put others through the same hell. This is the beauty of gagmail – all you have to do is press a button and you can distribute one to hundreds of others. These things spread like wildfire and they get noticed, a fact that surely has not escaped the attention of advertising agencies. The first sponsored gagmails cannot be far away.

In the meantime, the phenomenon continues. Wasting hundreds of man (or woman) hours. Abusing office equipment. Causing havoc for IT staff.

And it's wonderful. Every crap joke that takes half an hour to download, every lame list that clogs up our hard drives should be cherished because it is humanising technology. It's the digital equivalent of photocopying your backside. Grim sci-fi predictions of a future in which we are enslaved by technology will never come about as long as we retain our innate ability to drag every technological advance down to our own level.

So, if your boss discovers you downloading a 10Mb video clip of a urinating orang-utan on company time, just tell him to lay off. What you are doing is essential to the future well-being of mankind.

Patrick Burgoyne

http://mpfwww.jpl.nasa.gov/MPF/index1.html

NASA MARS PATHFINDER
Launch Date: 04 December 1996 UT 06:58
Arrival Date: 04 July 1997 UT 16:57
Launch Vehicle: Delta II

Crossing the 240,000-mile divide, Earth Man walked the lunar landscape on July 21, 1969 and stayed for eighty hours, at an estimated cost of $200,000 per minute. Above our heads, the expansion into outer space unknown continues. The recent orbital trip of the 77-year-old John Glenn signals corporate expansion will be directed towards the stratosphere.

Featuring a browsable online atlas of Mars, containing USGS maps and Viking Orbiter images, NASA's Pathfinder website shows the latest images of the planet captured through the robotic eye view of the Sojourner Rover. Densely detailed information is given on average Martian temperature, equatorial radius, escape velocity, specific missions and objectives, instruments and individual spacecraft – the hardware of Martian discovery. Application of digital technology at the source of these images allows subtle control of colour balance, contrast and density, in ways that surpass conventional analog darkroom techniques. The physics of human colour perception on planets other than Earth are more complex and subjective. Without an atmosphere, visible light becomes blinding.

Offering an aesthetics of space and the ultimate in landscape photography, these pictures eloquently describe new scale and alien surface.

'Our spaceships will have geometries which minimize frontal friction, channel incoming plasma flow with helical (centripetal) internal paths for burning, deflect external (centrifugal) paths for envelope-shaping, push against the background aether-field flow, and shield against internal radiation and magnetic accesses. We intend to share technology rather than burn bridges. In space, nobody can hear you violating copyright.'

Space Travel By Any Means Necessary! – The Fourth Annual Report of the Association of Autonomous Astronauts [June 1999]

'Inventions, the creations of scientists, are riddles which expand the field of the unknown.'
Paul Virilio, *Pure War*

'Any sufficiently advanced technology becomes indistinguishable from magic.'
Arthur C Clarke

Smart audio bugs, heavy-duty gelcams, sensors and detectors, pulleys, latches, priceless vials of programmed neural data. She ascended the diagrid shell structure of Super Terminal 1. On the surface of her spex, Roma's glowing fingertips whipped across the field of Shaun's vision, and pointed. 'Something's moving out there.' We had company.

'Having no material technology, the technology on Mars is based on thought and spirit. Their language and ways of communication are quite musical and melodic'
LBH-6251876: A Red Planet Compilation/Submerge 1999

'The Martian synthesises a cosmic disco that colonizes Mars in advance of the landing, so that if we come into contact with intelligent lifeforms from another planet we can talk on the same level'
Mike Banks, *Underground Resistance*

0.5 seconds of processed digisignal feedsforward a scene from an unknown future...

Deirdre Crowley

http://mpfwww.jpl.nasa.gov/MPF/index1.html

http://www.nsc.ru/lans/resource.html

Name the third largest city in Russia. Here is a clue: it is the capital of a territory that makes up around one-twelfth of the world's land surface. Time up. The answer is Novosibirsk, Siberia. I had reason to be there in person, so, faced with the absence of basic travel guidance in my local bookshop, I turned to the web. A simple search threw up more than 10,000 relevant sites: would I like to refine my search terms? No, I wouldn't, I didn't, and so I plunged in near the top of the list.

I entered this meta-site, an aggregator of content about Novosibirsk. I found that the city name means, literally, New Siberia, an unsought gift from the Communists in the 1920s to a growing town astride the river Ob. In subsequent five-year plans, Nature was pushed aside as lives were dedicated to building an industrial and academic centre that was, for many years, a closed city (and was also the centre for much of the thinking that went into perestroika). Around 1.6 million Siberians now live in the sprawling megalopolis, a network of locations so messily arranged that it takes around two hours to cross. I did not easily find the standard travel details I sought. I found this frustrating at first, but came to realise that I had travelled further into the minds and the dreams past and present of New Siberians than I could have hoped.

Now, some months on from the visit, I look back at the site and find it a remarkable document about a place, and a consciousness, that is fast-changing, even disappearing.

There is a fundamental difference between this and the Western model of the large internet site. These pages and this network are clearly not put together to serve the profit motive, nor are they for individuals' self-promotion. In fact, it is hard to pin down for what purpose they were assembled: they are post-communist but pre-capitalist, and they carry with them ill-defined hope. Behind the pages, somebody cares to make contact, and to make contact not just for themselves but for their people.

When I went to Novosibirsk, I could not buy a postcard in the hotel lobby: only alcohol, cigarettes and sex were on sale. On the web I was able to find virtual postcards... images celebrating sunset over nearby Lake Baikal, the monumental squares photographed in a favourable light, or the latest mammoth to be unfrozen. I could also dig deeper into the scientific quests that dominate Novosibirsk's cultural thought and reason to exist.

I could establish profound dialogues with scientists, if I wanted. Indeed, the more aspirational and intimate Novosibirsk existed, perhaps still exists, on the web, while a rather joyless place is available in reality. Perhaps there is a more substantial take on capitalism at work here than at first I thought.

Lewis Blackwell

http://www.protest.net

In *The Insider* (1999), Michael Mann's compelling film about corporate whistle-blower Jeffrey Wigand, Wigand and his family are described as ordinary people being asked to cope with extraordinary pressure, as they come up against the full force of corporate America. Wigand was the central witness in the law suits filed by the state of Mississippi and 49 other states against the tobacco industry, which, in 1998, resulted in a $246 billion settlement.

We can't all be Jeffrey Wigand, but we can make a difference – this seems to be the philosophy behind the invigorating website called protest.net.com. Protest.net is the cyberspace successor to the pamphleteer, or as the *New York Times* put it, 'Protest portals unite activists under one URL'.

Ideas and issues flow thick and fast: one click takes you from 'about Protest.net' to 'Znet', which provides a global calendar of protests, benefits meetings and conferences. It gives the who, what, where and when – pages of information for the backpacker with attitude. Each day, Znet selects global issues being debated by non-government organisations in Europe and beyond, for your consideration and comment – not your credit card number. Protest.net.com may lack the on-screen humour of Michael Moore, but more than makes up for that in depth and flow of information.

The site includes an activists' handbook, full of quotes from Mahatma Gandhi, Malcolm X, Martin Luther King, Tom Hayden and Joan Baez. Useful tips are dispensed to the would-be protestor: how to handle the media, how to publish a newsletter and advice on being a home-based activist. A damning article on 'The ten worst multinational companies of 1999' starts with a little help from Dickens: 'It was the best of times, it was the worst of times' – sentiments echoed in the Noam Chomsky archive, where you can download a range of audio interviews from the great man himself. To show that activists do have a sense of fun, there is a link to Urban75 webzine, which gives information on drugs, raves and features a refreshingly un-PC section called 'punch 'em', where you can give your least favourite celebrity or politician a good old cyberslap in the face.

Protest.net's directory has links to like-minded sites, such as the feminist newsletter Maximag, the anti-TV group White Dot and Working for Digital Freedom Network, who publish banned, censored and sensitive political documents from all over the world. But for a simple, wholesome statement of intent, the mantra of the Mad Anarchist Bakers is hard to beat: 'Make pies, not war'.

Karen Alexander

A net is a collection of holes held together by string. The net is a collection of holes held together (and torn apart) by links. Like *Six Degrees of Separation*, whereby we've all slept with someone who's slept with someone etc, with Kevin Bacon. Or was it Spacey?

Who is at the centre? Or was it originally a queue, with Kevin at the head? Our thirst for a rationale,

a cause and effect, renders every netsurf a miserable, frustrating experience. The chain snaps and fragments like spun sugar. Kevin is nowhere in sight.

Where did it begin? Who is No.1? If I follow every link after viewing every page on every site, how wide is a moonbeam? Who holds the record for the longest continuous surf? Who has a guestbook with more entries than there are words in the Bible? And this frustration – does this drive the search onward, outward? Or inward?

The further this non-search takes us, the deeper the voyeurism. And one surfer's voyeurism is ineluctably another server's fetishism. Just how much do I need to know about the birds landing in a Cheshire garden? Like some passive partner in an eternal orgy, I never wanted to go this far: to penetrate the exposed psyche of a man who is trapped, like the eunuch in the

harem – someone who can watch, but cannot do.

Those who have come through the catechism and emerged on the other side with little more than imaginary weals will appreciate the comparison between the size of a web-page and the depth of the creator's guilt. Guilt – and its soulmate shame – provokes an insatiable need for expiation through confession. Confession may be a private matter, so-called, a one-on-one. But how much more soothing the shame, how much harder hitting the guilt when the confession is taken beyond, when it cries out for approbation through theatrical self-humiliation. Hey, look at my site, I have something to admit. Sign my guestbook, and give me one more statistic to add to the mnemonic of my url.

Come by, and witness my ecstatic torture. Examine the life of an un-named archivist. Touch me in cyberspace and prove we are not alone.

David Roper

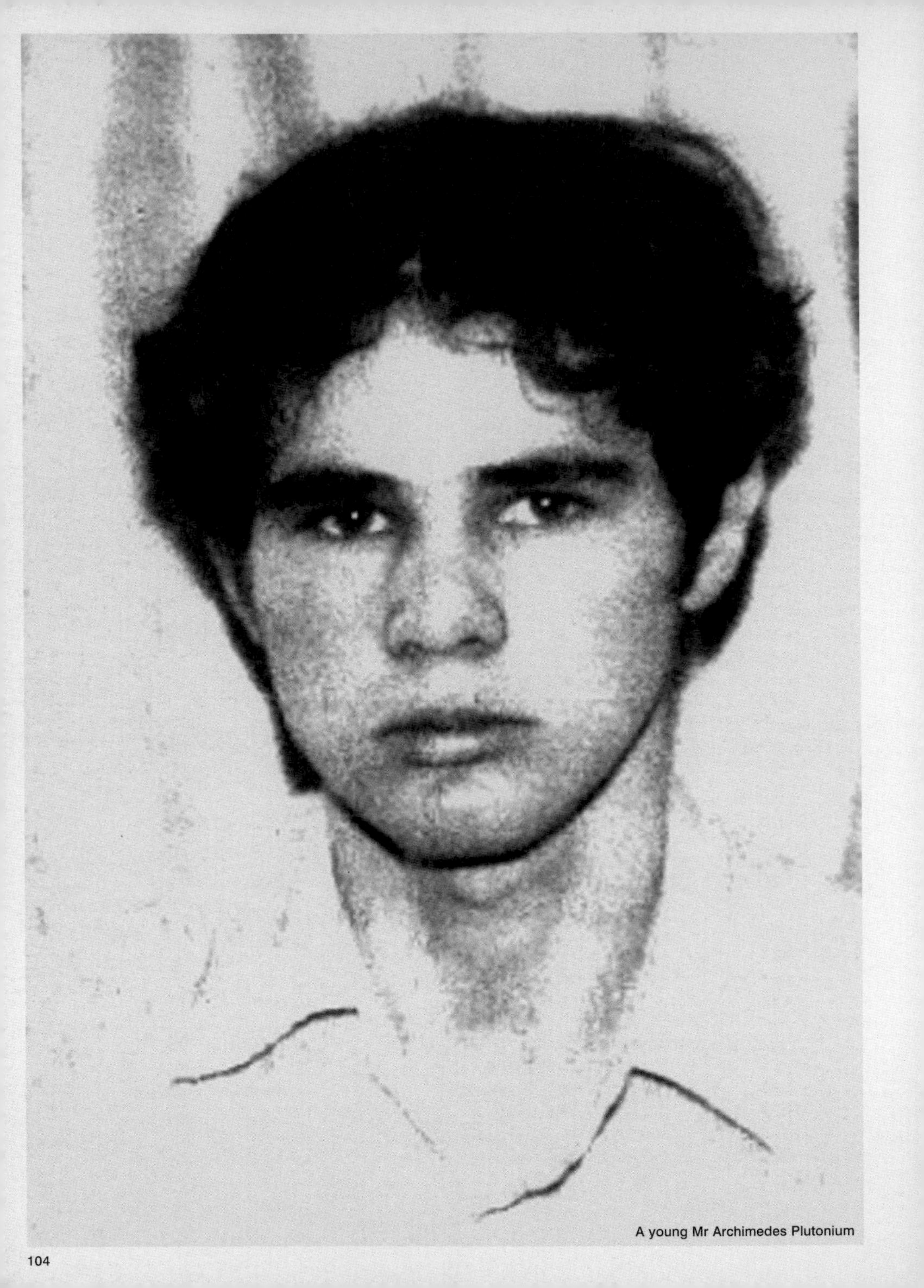
A young Mr Archimedes Plutonium

http://www.galstar.com/~ichudov/ppl/ap/index.html

'Mr Abian has become somewhat of a legend as the man who wanted to blow up the moon. But to his family and friends he was a normal man who liked Beethoven, Picasso and chocolate eclairs.' This death notice for a man who believed the answer to Earth's environmental and social problems was to nuke the moon is respectfully reprinted in the autobiography of Archimedes Plutonium, at www.galstar.com/~ichudov/ppl/ap/index.html. Mr Plutonium has a theory, too: the Plutonium Atom Totality Theory. Plutonium (symbol PU; atomic number 94) is his god, and his theory states that the entire universe is in fact a plutonium atom. This eccentric proposition has since ballooned on his truly encyclopaedic website to include theories on everything: physics, astronomy, psychology, an 'optimal strategy' for playing the stock market and poker, an ongoing autobiography, movie ideas (watch out for *Lady Chatterly's Fusion* – she's presumably played by a plutonium blonde), and even rewrites of Christmas carols and hymns. All together now, to the tune of He's Got The Whole World In His Hands:

'It's Got the Whole Observable Universe in its 94th Electron. PU has our Whole Observable Universe in its 94th Electron.'

His site's unmemorable address and lack of flashing lights to greet passing surfers show supreme self-confidence. This is one man's legacy: peruse it if you will. Of course he is obsessive, deluded and probably lonely and his creation is self-indulgent beyond belief. But it's impossible not to admire the sheer enormity of his task. Get beyond the nonsensical theories and it's hard not to be intrigued by what sort of a man lies behind it. Some of the writing is surprisingly moving as he recalls his poor upbringing as a German exile in America, and includes a photograph of the gravestone of his mother, lamenting the fact that it is the only picture he has of her. He claims he was a teacher, was fired from the US Navy, then became an organic fruit farmer before ending up as a dishwasher at a small Ivy League college in New Hampshire.

At the end of 1999, aged 49, he embarked on a tour of America, visiting the sites of famous scientific achievements, and has plans to head on to Europe to do the same. He has an apparently endless curiosity but what is lacking is any sense of proportion or of intentional humour. There are laughs, though, in his descriptions of his US odyssey, as if he were seeing through the eyes of a child or an alien the Greyhound buses, the washing and drying facilities at restaurants en route, and fruit. 'Today I tried something new and delicious. I bought 4 from a street vendor. They are called "satsuma".' Or his musing on the apparent lack of purpose of the blisters on his feet: 'Water blisters are counterexample to Darwin Evolution theory.'

I look forward to reading his reactions to Europe, that distant continent where, he fears, a lack of computer links will prevent him continuing his work. Unsurprisingly, Archimedes Plutonium is convinced he will be seen as a legend whose name will be in encyclopaedias in years to come. Until then, he offers a full transcript of one fleeting appearance on local TV news. For the moment, he is just a peculiar man with a liking for Peter Gabriel, hand dryers – and the satsuma.

Andrew Preston

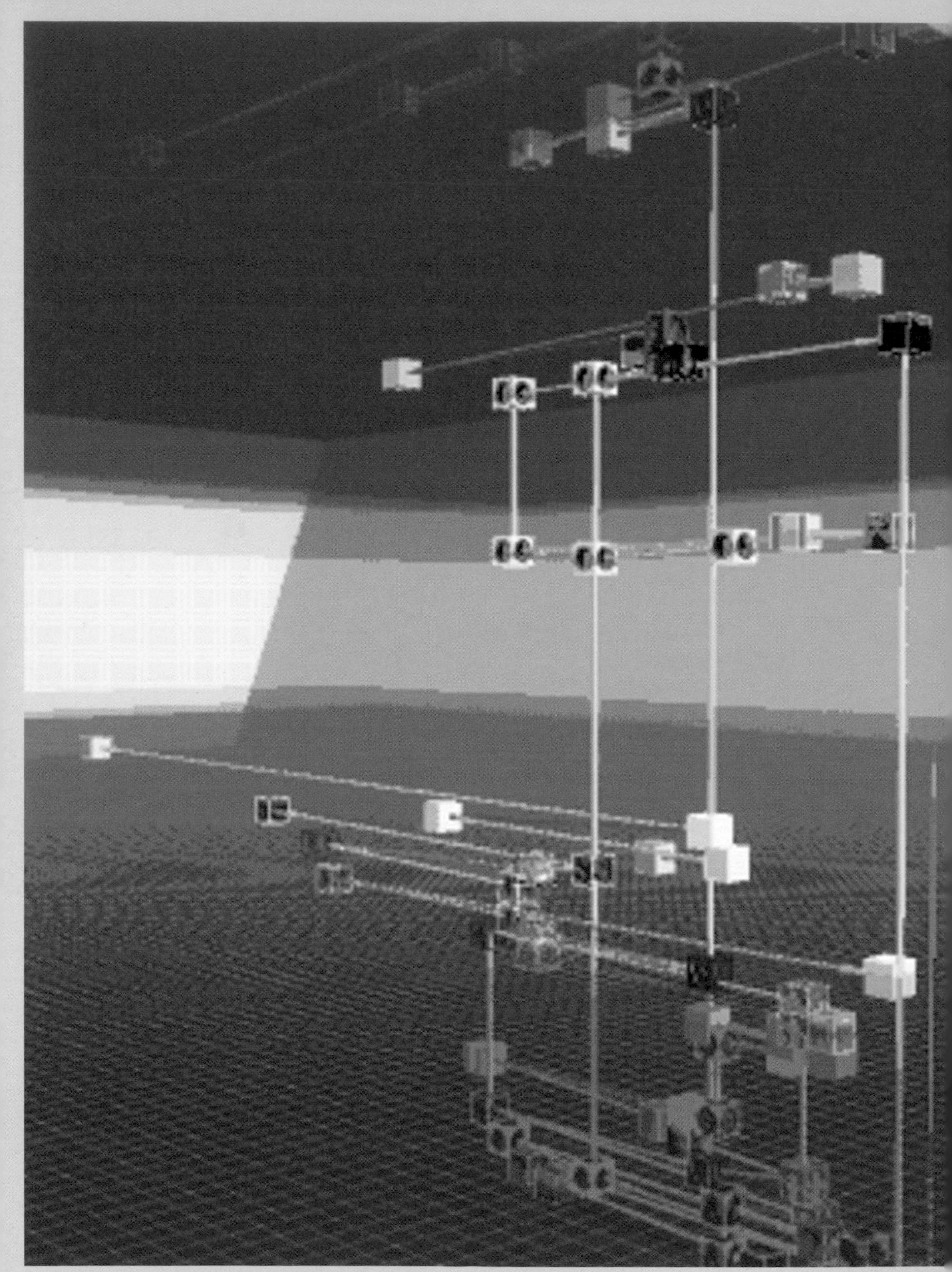

http://www.geog.ucl.ac.uk/casa/martin/atlas

We call it cyberspace, but it isn't. It isn't space at all: it is cables and electronic signals, spaces and flows, screens and servers and keyboards, and so, trying to represent the reality of the world-wide web in two dimensions is a strange enterprise; strange and sometimes extraordinarily beautiful.

Maps are, by definition, a subjective version of the past – they represent someone's fixed view of reality as it was at one point in time. These are supposed to be real maps of the present, attempts to pin down a very rapidly shifting pattern of connections, as if the London Underground were being rebuilt every night and extended so that you could go from Pimlico to Irkutsk (change at Victoria, Dover Western Docks and Brno). Every trick of two-dimensional representation is used – colour, shape, contour, shading and perspective – in the collection assem bled by the Department of Geography at University College London.

There are the strange empty landscapes of the Harmony Internet browser, evoking Dali or De Chirico; the eerie Populated Information Terrains or Tim Bray's oddly shaped figures straight from Magritte. The Urlgraph by Kevin Palfreyman is more towards the conceptual end of the spectrum, strange lines connecting odd names across a curiously blank grid. Emmanuel Frécon's WebPath, developed at the charmingly named Distributive Collaborative Environments group, is like a bafflingly complex construction toy; others are like wiring diagrams, Spirograph on speed or just prosaic flow charts. But perhaps the most mystical and mystifying are Sarah Fabrikant's spatial landscapes, smooth, featureless yet as loaded with information as an Ordnance Survey Landranger.

If you drop in on Ms Fabrikant's web page, you can immerse yourself in her explanations of the use of spatial metaphors, from the easy-to-handle idea of the 'desktop' to the arcana of 'proceeding-article-landscapes' and 'access-frequency-surfaces'. Maybe you'll want to go on to read Menno-Jan Kraak & Alan MacEachren's Visualization for Exploration of Spatial Data; perhaps lurch, increasingly dazzled, down the link to Karma vl, 'an application for modelling, manipulation and analysis of two and three-dimensional spatial (GIS) data within a Virtual Reality environment', designed to model 'large infrastructure works in The Netherlands'.

It is at this stage that the reality component of what you're looking at becomes a little difficult to grasp, and you have to start reminding yourself that these are just computer programmes that change the colour of little electronic thingies on a television screen in a particularly ingenious fashion, modelled on someone's idea of something that isn't really there. Just as art is really only colours on a piece of canvas. Or, perhaps, you will recall Jorge Luis Borges, who describes an empire which sets out to draw up a map so detailed that it ends up exactly covering the territory.

Baudrillard used this as a way of talking about simulation and suchlike. But go back to Borges' original, which is far more playful, more original and amusing. Borges would have loved these Dutch cyber-geographers, the Fabrikants, Kraaks and Palfreymans; perhaps he even imagined them. Perhaps these curious spinning wheels of web connections are his, or were created by some Borges imposter with a Powerbook. Perhaps they don't even really exist, whatever that means.

Andrew Marshall

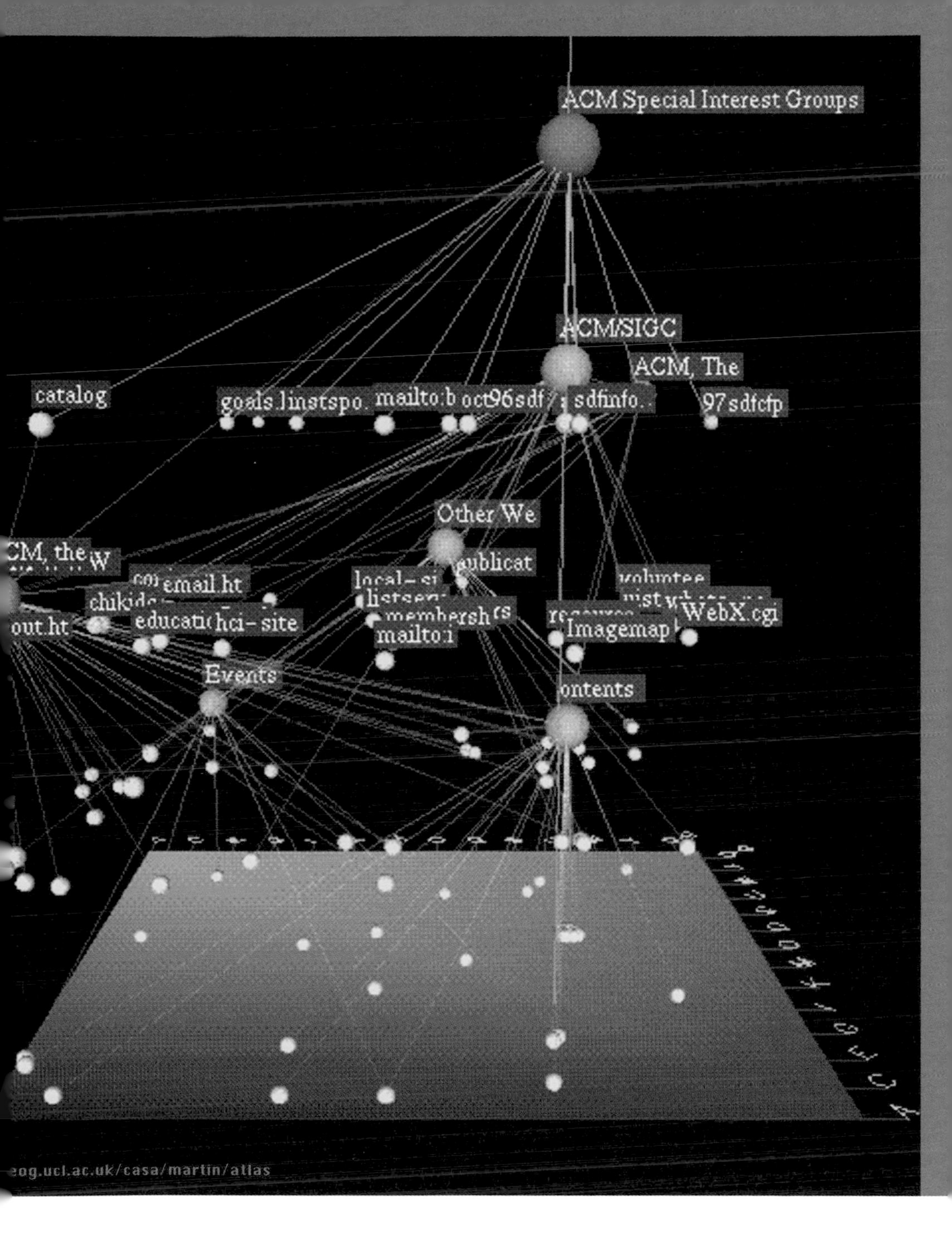
ACM Special Interest Groups
ACM/SIGC
ACM, The
catalog
mailto:b
oct96sdf
sdfinfo..
97sdfcfp
Other We
email.ht
hci-site
out.ht
WebX.cgi
Imagemap
mailto:i
Events
ontents
eog.ucl.ac.uk/casa/martin/atlas

http://www.celgene.com

For those who espouse high moral and ethical standards, some websites provoke nothing but disgust and anger. Although it is free of violence and pornography, I imagine that, for many, www.celgene.com, too, is deeply offensive.

This is the web page for the US-based Celgene Corporation, a pharmaceutical company at the cutting edge of the biochemical revolution – a revolution not only in biochemistry but also of stocks and shares. Celgene Corp is yet another biochemical company whose promises alone have valued it at billions of dollars. Click on Investor Relations and you'll get a detailed profile of the corporation's stock price, updated every 15 minutes. Click on Who's Who and you'll get a short bio of the ten or so men – and they are all men – entrusted to develop, manufacture and market the drugs and agrochemicals that will take us into the 21st century. And click on Employment Opportunities to see how you, too, could become part of a cutting edge corporation championing the dubious cause of genetic and biochemical engineering.

In fact, it doesn't take long to understand that this is a website designed for stocks and shares analysts; it's a cursory glance at Celgene Corp, its products, its mission statements, its managers and its share price. Its message is clear: invest. For Celgene Corp is the future of medicine. It promises to cure our incurable diseases and to provide us with handsome profits at the same time. Health, wealth and happiness all in one – at least, for those who can afford it. So is it any wonder that the NHS in Britain is fighting a losing battle? And to complicate matters further, Celgene is the company that continues to manufacture and market Thalomid, the new name for Thalidomide, pariah drug of the medical establishment. For many, it doesn't get any more offensive than www.celgene.com.

But for me, there's another side to this coin. For sites like www.celgene.com are invaluable for sufferers of chronic and incurable diseases, many of whom are constantly searching the net for information on new treatments and breakthrough discoveries. Believe it or not, Thalidomide is the precursor to a brand new family of drugs called Selective Cytokine Inhibitory Drugs (SelCIDs). Although these are early days, SelCIDs already promise to be the most effective weapon we have in the fight against diseases as varied as leprosy, rheumatoid arthritis, Crohn's disease, many AIDS related illnesses and even some cancers. Click on Products and you will see details of Celgene's revolutionary drug development programme. Click on Balancing Benefits and Risks and you have a considered argument revolving around issues of safety and quality of life. Click on Prescribing Information and you have access to detailed facts about how the drug works and how it should be used. And even though it's over most of our heads, the point is you have access to information that has hitherto been the domain of doctors. When was the last time your GP had either the time, the inclination or the knowledge to explain even half of the above?

For me, these positive aspects of celgene.com represent the internet at its best. Maybe it's a cliché, but knowledge is power and empowerment is what the 'information superhighway' promised to give us.

As a sufferer of Crohn's disease, I can now walk into my consultant and demand to talk about Thalidomide as a potential treatment for my condition – with the confidence that I know what I'm talking about. No longer am I at the mercy of apathetic doctors who can't be bothered to keep up with developments and are mostly concerned with their impending retirement. Sad to say, it happens. So, at its best, www.celgene.com gives me back a sense of control over the path my health care will take.

The other day, I walked into my doctor and asked about an important new drug called Infliximab that limits the production of Tumour Necrosis Factor. Unfortunately, my doctor had never heard of it.

Chris Symes

http://www.sensorium.org

What kind of pleasure have you received from the internet? And what have you used it for? To get some information about gardening or other hobbies? To buy some luxurious underwear from a mail-order company? You certainly don't need to go to a far-off library or walk through a crowded department store any more. But is the internet worth the cost of your computer? Or the trouble and time that it takes for you to download the necessary software? After this, if you reach a website that is filled with worthless boasting, or an 'out of stock' message, you might regret that you didn't go drinking with your friends instead.

www.sensorium.org may give you an opportunity to realise again the *raison d'être* of the internet, if you are fed up with its teething troubles. The organisers of this site are trying to produce a kind of institution similar to an aquarium or a planetarium, to make you aware of the broad expanse of the world and the feeling that we are living together on the same planet, even if we are speaking different languages or separated by oceans.

'Breathing Earth' is one of their experiments. Here, you can see loop animations made by picture frames visualised from data of disatrophism (movement of the earth's crust). They receive the disatrophism data twice a day from all over the earth through the internet. Then they programme the most recent two weeks' pictures to run as animation. The size of the swell translates as the amount of movement of the earth's crust.

The Asian area that includes Japan is well known to be subject to frequent earthquakes, large and small. But we Japanese go about our everyday lives unaware that so many earthquakes happen around us. Using the site, you realise that our planet is alive with a throbbing pulse.

Another experiment, called 'Night and Day' is, according to sensorium, 'a natural time clock using the visualisation of natural sights' – as opposed to 'clock time', the social notion of time we usually use, which is prescribed artificially. A circle consisting of 24 pictures is sent by web cams from different longitudes around the world through the internet. It allows you to discover where the sun is rising and where night is falling simply by looking at the pictures, without using a clock and without calculating time differences.

There are other interesting experiments in sensorium.org. What they are trying to achieve with this website is a recognition of your position as a part of the whole world or the galaxy. Using information that is the essence of the internet and translating it into different information is a renewal of the way we see the world – a method that the Japanese have used for a long time.

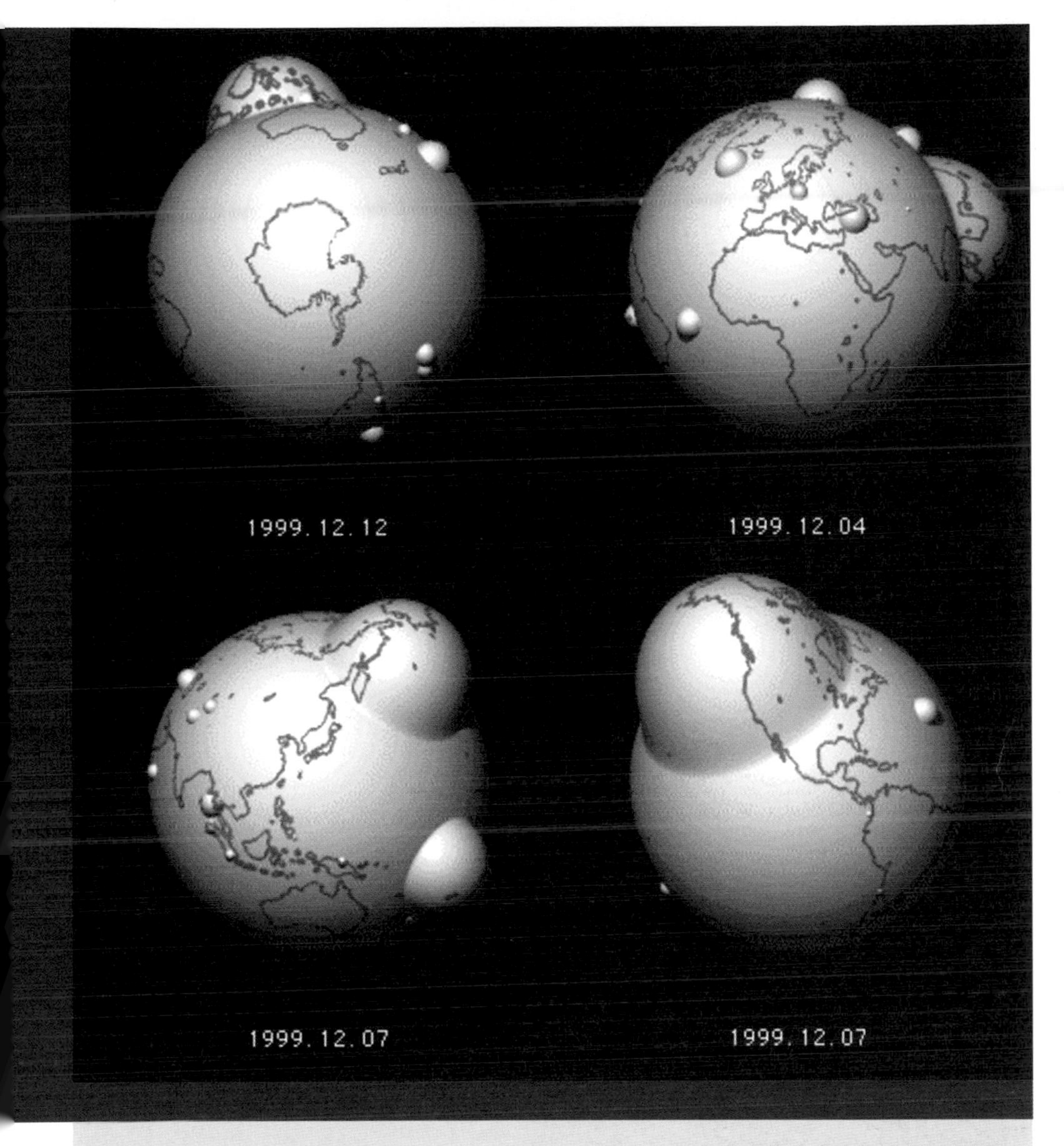

In the Japanese tea ceremony, the host must arrange the equipment and decoration to give an impression of coolness in summer and of warmth in winter. The effect is gained by visual means – so, an iron kettle warmer is used in summer and a pottery kettle warmer in winter. The Japanese used to employ all the senses to capture a view of the world. In the same way, the organisers of sensorium are trying to express a view of the world using both the technology of the internet and their own culture, philosophy and senses.

Naoko Hasegawa

http://www.st.rim.or.jp/~flui/bk/baka_home.html

Many magazines have made special features on Japanese architecture/living in the last few months. To talk about architecture is becoming a petit boom among non-professionals.

Of course, there has been interest in modern architecture for a long time because we've never stopped building since the Japanese high-growth period in the sixties. In the seventies and eighties the numbers of buildings increased and didn't start to decline till the peak of the construction boom in the early nineties. Architecture grew like creatures and covered all Japan. The growth kept going even after 1991, when we recognised we would go into a recession.

One of the most significant changes during the last decade has been the shortage of funds for new buildings. Gigantic architecture used to be built amazingly quickly, perhaps only a year or two after planning at the economic peak. But now it takes much longer to collect funds. It causes a design time lag; many of the new buildings were designed in the early nineties and reflect the era's decorative style. For instance, a huge building in Aoyama completed a few months ago, which is famous for its tenant Gucci shop: from a distance the building looks like a Japanese tomb, with its polished grey stone material, and the details look like Roman ruins.

Another notable change is that people are cool about new buildings. Perhaps since Starck's Asahi Beer building, people have got bored. No matter how gigantic, weirdly designed or hi-tech, new buildings never astonish us as they used to.

The website Baka Kenchiku Tanteidan (stupid architecture detectives) criticises weird design architecture. The targets that are listed number 11 so far. The site's author Mr Frui says the conditions of Baka Kenchiku (stupid architecture) are: its form is strange enough to cause laughter; its contents and purpose are incoherent; it is alienated from its surroundings; it is artistic but fishy; its design is a copy; it is an eyesore, etc.

Moreover, he argues that there are several types of Baka Kenchiku, which can be categorised... Atelier type: based on complex concepts but ignore their surroundings. Yankee type: the Japanese word 'Yankee' is hard to translate. It describes Japanese hot-rodders and motorcycle gangs, which are a very original Japanese group, but (maybe because they have rarely benefited from further education?) are hardly recognised as a culture. The first purpose of the Yankee type buildings is to show off and to appeal loudly to the public. They are often found among pachinco arcade, love hotels and nouveau-riche houses.

Reckless section chief type: these are public facilities – for instance, stations, public phones, toilets and schools. Civil servants cudgelled their

brains to make adorable architecture but the results are like kids' toys (you may find them in Britain such as the Millennium Dome in London and the Pop Museum in Sheffield).

The author and his friends visit such architecture and record their conversations. They are neither architecture critics nor professionals in the field but simply represent the general public. That's why it is fun to read their impudent talk. It isn't frequently updated but they continuously and enthusiastically seek new targets. It's a pity that there are some construction problems in this site, such as pictures covering some of the text. Or is it case of a Baka Kenchiku?

Chi-haru Watabe

http://www.sorabji.com/livewire/payphones/project.html

When I was a student, I shared a house with, amongst others, a punctilious, thoroughly reasonable girl who decided that the best way to divide up the bill for the communal phone was to have a neatly ruled book into which we would all write the details of every call made – by whom, where to, at what time, for how long; there was even, God help us, a column in which to write down the charge band used.

At the end of term, Lady Sensible would sit herself down, tot up all the calls and issue us with our personalised bills. In order to spice up her task, my friend Q and I played the immensely enjoyable late-night game of picking the code for Guinea Bissau, Ecuador or Macau out of the phone book, adding a random six or seven-figure number and seeing who we got. Waiters in Poland, a nurse in Hong Kong, the switchboard supervisor of PNG Electrics, the Papua New Guinea electricity board – we heard them all. The theme was international friendship, the joy of strange voices, and pages of 45-second phone calls to add up.

The Payphone Project at sorabji.com panders to the same infantile impulse to telephone complete strangers, providing thousands of numbers around the world and photographs of many of the payphones in question.

Contributions come from all over, but there is no payphone hunter more dogged than 'Rex', from Kansas, who has page after page to himself. Rex's photographs capture the empty horror of the mid-West – payphones standing proud in just-so streets and never a human being in sight. The main street of Kanopolis (785 472 8903) is a vision of bleakness that should be studied by anyone who claims their town is boring (though Rex does his best to sell us Kansas in his brief comments – 'I believe Kanopolis still has an operational drive-in theatre', he adds, optimistically).

(801) 237 2085 Courtesy phone, Rice Eccles Stadium, Salt Lake City, Utah

But Rex's finest excursion took him across the border into Oklahoma – scary! – in search of one of America's remotest payphones, which he'd been told about by his brother-in-law. He knows roughly where he's going, but stops at Buster's bar in Sun City, Oklahoma (photograph supplied) for precise directions. There, Jim, a pumper who checks oil wells and knows this territory like the back of his beer mat, tells him the magic phone is on the Z Bar Ranch, out in 'open range' country. Sun City is the last town Rex will pass through for 14 miles.

The quest is successful. Out in the middle of nowhere, on the brow of a small hill, stands a telegraph pole, shaped like an old rugged cross. Fixed to it is a Radio Shack phone and a number. Rex picks it up. The line is dead. But if it ever gets reconnected, you can call a cowboy on 316 886 5205.

Richard Preston

Midtown Manhattan Bar

www.sorabji.com/livewire/payphones/project.html

http://www.samplenet.co.uk

So now we've got the internet and access to everything. Now it's all global. Now you can download bits of music and make some other bits of music...

Poking around the web looking for audio samples to satisfy my curiosity took several search engines and so much time that I could have learned, rehearsed and recorded the complete works of Sonic Youth. Eventually, I came across samplenet.co.uk, offering a small selection of licence-free samples – drums, guitars, vocals, synths, orchestral, etc. In theory, you use them in your piece of music and watch the result scale the charts, without fear of James Brown and his bunch of funky drummers turning up on your doorstep demanding recompense (or worse). The reality, however, is a bunch of cheesy synth pads and a girl moaning 'AH LERV TERCHING MAHSELF'.

Making music is really about more than this. Remote and lonely music-making usually makes for remote and lonely music. But opting for the sampled jigsaw-puzzle school of music is a defeat – and, frankly, the notion of building a guitar riff from downloaded wave files is too stupid even to contemplate. Remember the old punk diagram? This is an E chord, this is an F chord, this is a G chord – now form a band. The formula here is more like: this is a website, this is a hard drive... oh, never mind, let's look at some porn. Hardly has the same cultural implications, does it?

So... what if you make your piece of music using this crap, then somebody gets hold of it (probably because you uploaded it on to one of those free music sites) and it gets used everywhere from Hotlunch.com to the American Airlines TV ad campaign and that's supposed to be fine, because nothing belongs to anyone any more, does it? What d'you do then? Oh, I forgot, you can't hear me because you're busy screaming into that cushion.

The synth-biased feel of many of these clips put me off and got me thinking about quality. Clearly, the hope that you can pull down prepacked pieces and assemble anything other than off-the-peg mood music is a mistake... it won't be real music, like porn ain't real sex. Don't Sample – Example. Folks can tell.

Andy Martin

http://www.drbukk.com/gmhom/gmindex.html

It is one of today's greatest mysteries. What psychic need – or is it simple financial incentive? – has pulled the dysfunctional, the fuck-ups, the fucked-over and the absurdly obese out of America's trailer parks to reveal their shabbiest secrets and evidence of poor hair care regimes to audiences of baying, frothing peers and a voyeuristic TV nation that points, jeers and grimaces? Is an awful kind of validation on offer? Or whopping pay cheques? Who knows, but it has made *The Jerry Springer Show* and other daytime talk shows horribly compulsive viewing. Cinema has also explored and exploited an imagined white trash world where domestic violence, abuse, alcoholism, ignorance, incest, homicidal scheming and atrocious personal hygiene are commonplace. But the internet offers up a more sophisticated, more generous view of the people of the trailer parks.

One such anthropological resource is Great Mobile Homes of Mississippi, a tribute to the 'vernacular architecture' of that state and a hymn to the joys of 'affordable living and creative landscapes'. The site offers a step-by-step, lavishly illustrated guide to creating the perfect trailer-based estate. Dereliction and debris are everything for a trailer of distinction. Shabby add-ons, yard junk and pet litter (indoors and out) are essential. Numerous long-immobile automobiles are also must-haves, as is a fully functional Trans-Camaro, a mutational vehicle usually including various bits of a Firebird and/or a Camaro and/or a Trans-Am. A giant satellite dish is also a key architectural feature for the finer 'manufactured home'.

Are they having a laugh? Well, of course they are and the most entertaining element of the site is the impressive collection of e-mails, misspellings and all, it has generated. Many of them are from former or current trailer folk willing to laugh along and bring their own tales of degradation and horror. Some of these are simple if sneering fun and some are truly sad and disturbing. Even more disturbing, though, are the messages from recalcitrant rednecks who argue that a home in a trailer park will always be preferable to living in the 'projects with crackers' and that armed insurrection against liberals, blacks, Hispanics and others who threaten the White Southern way is just around the corner. For many Mississippians, the Civil War is clearly not over.

You have to steer yourself to Great Mobile Homes of Mississippi through drbukk.com, an expansive site dedicated to a range of orthodontic horrors currently enjoying cult status in the States. This range of carefully catalogued comedy teeth is more proof that many American urbanites remain convinced that inbred hillbillies with terrible deformities run rampant beyond the city walls. Funny as this is, you do begin to understand why Southern country folk can get a little prickly about smart-ass Yankees.

Nick Compton

http://www.drbukk.com/gmhom/gmindex.html

http://www.xvt.com/users/kevink/silo

If you are fascinated with the dark places of the earth, then climb down the stairs of this 1960s Titan I missile silo to the thousands of feet of tunnels that lie somewhere below the American plains. When it was operational, only a handful of people would have been here; now, some 250,000 people have visited its corridors.

In constructing their site, Kevin Kelm and David Rodenbaugh have kept a sense of the mystery and danger of their original, illegal expedition. These are dark, cavernous spaces, filled with graffiti, crumbling masonry, loops of wire that now go nowhere. The passage from room to room is made with graphics and photographs, while you speculate on the purposes of those who once lurked here, waiting for the end of the world. From the silo's giant launch tubes, three missiles would have been launched across the Arctic Circle to Russia, the inhabitants supposedly safe, far below the ground. The floors are mounted on giant springs to absorb blasts – but then, as one American general once put it: if you're in the crater, you're in the crater.

There are plenty of sites devoted to the underground – catacombs, shelters, fortresses, caves and other hidden places – and to Cold War arcana. There are guides to restoring your bunker (most are now decommissioned and available for private occupation) that tell you how to turn a hole in the ground into a desirable, if sepulchral home ('The Most Unique Real Estate You May Ever Own').

The appeal of the underground on the net is obvious: it is intertwined with the technology's own labyrinthine nature, and the fascination with concealment, conspiracy and secrecy (some of those missile silos are said to be inhabited by American militia groups).

But there is a deeper irony here: that these missile silos were created to carry out a war of indescribable violence, and so was the internet. It began with a need to create a communication technology that could carry on after a nuclear strike – that would allow information to be routed even when telephone exchanges were smoking ruins. The Pentagon's DARPANET was the great-great grandfather of the system that now allows us to download pictures of pop stars nude. It was designed to evade control, to seek ways around information blockages, because it was supposed to survive the end of the world.

In the same way, the nuclear catacombs were dug deep and scattered across the loneliest parts of America, to evade detection and make it impossible to knock out the country's nuclear capability with one blow. These dank bunkers are the unlikely cousins of the internet; both are children of the Armageddon that never took place.

Andrew Marshall

http://www.disinfo.com

This is the 'subculture search engine', the database you turn to when you want to work your way into the dark underbelly of the news; to that seedy underworld of conspiracy – or so disinfo.com would have us believe – that's carefully hidden from public scrutiny. We're talking big time conspiracy: governments, Christian Fascists, Televangelists, extraterrestrials, US Secessionists and Technosurrealists, the lot. Don't be deceived by the manipulative spiel served up on the TV. They're probably in it, too. There's a tough world out there and mad, bad people are out to get you. You might think that the Iron Curtain has been drawn back, but you'd be wrong. Only one force can save you. The disinformation website.

The self-proclaimed purpose of disinfo.com is to expose the truth that only rarely slips through the 'crack of the corporate owned media conglomerates'. Under 'Propaganda' the visitor is offered a range of media manipulations that extends from 'Biometrics' to 'The Tobacco War', 'CIA Crack Connection', 'Prozac' and 'The Federal Reserve'. In 'Revolutionaries' the visitor is invited to explore the mind and work of Philip K. Dick ('one of the most "out there" writers of all times' for those who haven't heard of him) among a motley crew of subversives that includes Jesus (the real Jesus, that is), Allen Ginsberg, William Burroughs and Gurdjieff. In 'Counterculture' we are cautioned against the 'outrageous sites lurking in the belly of the Internet Beast'. As the language intimates, this is an abracadabra world of beasts and maidens and knights in shining armour. The site revels in those very conspiracies it purports to rage against.

It isn't a subtle message, but it's one that has been hammered out with a zealousness that begins to make even the most open-minded browser uncomfortable. If you hang around conspirators for too long, you begin to sound like one. The visitor enters the well-designed and user friendly site to choose from a list of options that includes 'propaganda', 'revolutionaries', 'censorship', 'counterculture', 'counterintelligence' and 'newspeak'. In case it should have escaped us, we're reminded that 'information is power'. Although we're spared a lengthy Foucauldian disquisition on 'the archaeology of knowledge', the site directs the browser to an extra-mural session on Znet to hear what Noam Chomsky and Edward Said have to say on the Kosovo crisis.

Meanwhile we learn that much of the site's 'alternative' news is gleaned from CNN and *Time* magazine, while a snappy ad entreats the browser to drop into the Headshop and pick up a copy of Throbbing Gristle's Greatest Hits at $12.78. And why not throw some 'Disinfo Gear' into the trolley while you're at it – say a T-shirt or a coffee mug? All major credit cards are accepted in the 'store'. It's so easy! The disinfo.com message is that you have your cake and eat it. So long, of course, as you 'get off your butt' and sign up to disinformation: the truth is out there with a free laptop for those who subscribe.

Shannan Peckham

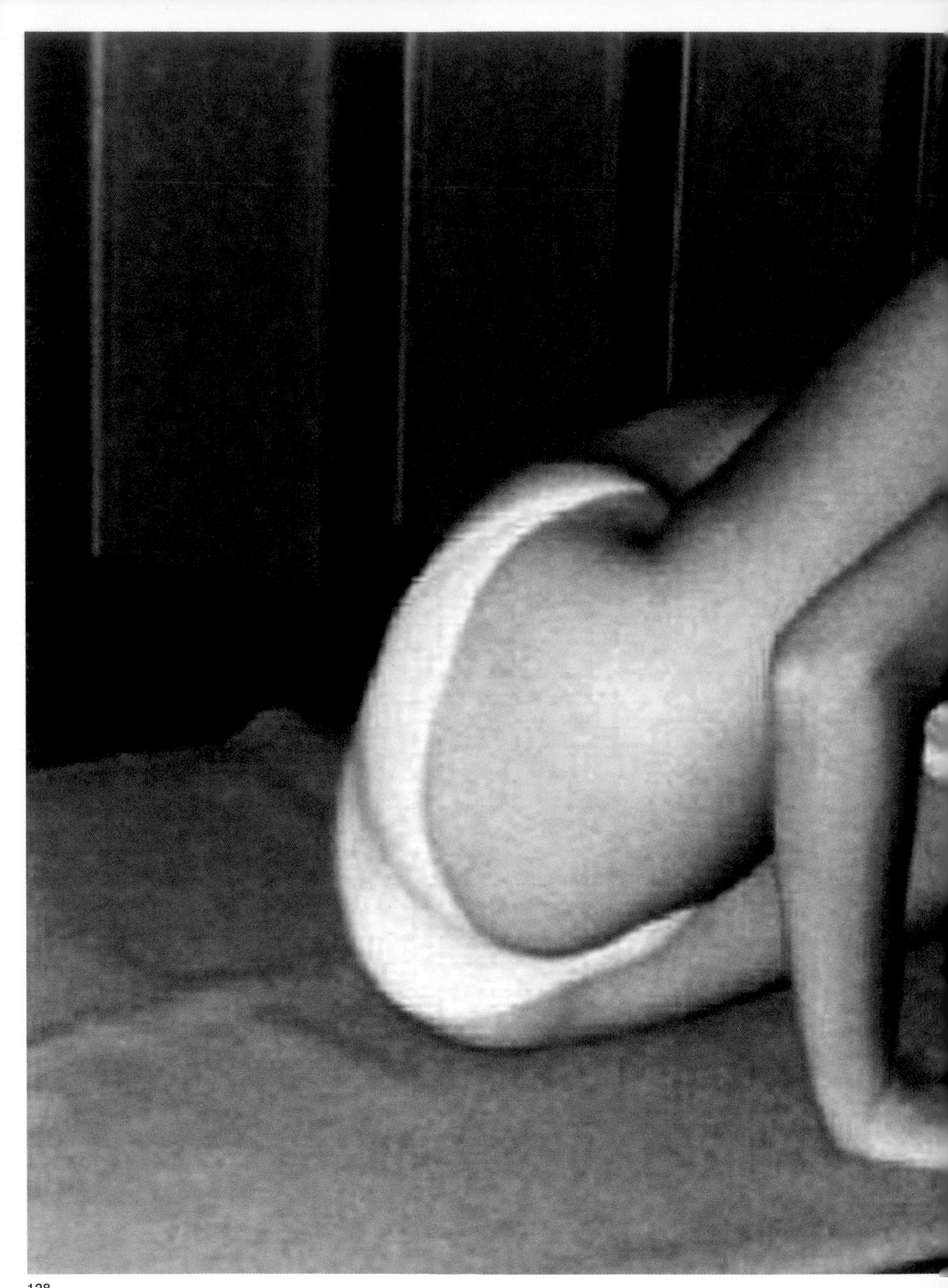

http://www.contortion
homepage.com

http://www.contortionhomepage.com

Coney Island, long a ghost town of a fun fair, seems to have found a new home on the web. The Contortion Home Page celebrates, as it says, 'those who take their physical abilities to the highest levels'. Some of the people pictured and described here are gymnasts or dancers, people in tights or tracksuits. But click a little further and the full circus comes into view: Elizabeth, the Polish front and back bender, clad in white underwear and rubberised so that the back of her head is flat against her spine; Ula, her compatriot, who can do 270-degree splits; Clifton, an impossibly bendy man in a unitard. The performers range from elegant to excessive: some are just slightly wonky ballerinas, others are proudly freakish – sideshow heroes and showbiz stars. At times, despite your awe and amazement, you can't help thinking that there is something mildly pornographic about the site – there are some male 'benders', but it's mostly full of girls in scanty clothes, with names like 'Ruby Ring' and 'Rose Zone', stretching into wild, undreamed-of positions.

Ron Dwight, whose photographic collection of contortionists is available on a set of 4 CD-Roms, has amassed 24,000 images over the years (50 copies of the first CD have been sold so far). The website, which is put together by Phil Silverback and Tige Young, is aimed at 'contortion enthusiasts' – but who, other than themselves and Ron Dwight, are these? It seems like an art from another age – there are photographs here of a 1950s contortionist, and an article reprinted from a Minneapolis newspaper of 1935 which shows x-rays of 'Miss Barlow', an acrobatic vamp. And many contortionists can't work for long – they lose their suppleness as their bones become brittle (only April Tatro's mother, who has appeared on Oprah Winfrey's show, is still winding her legs around her neck at the age of 86). How many people, one wonders, will turn up to 'ICC 2000', the International Contortion Convention, to be held in Las Vegas this September?

But anyone who has doubts that contortion is an art form should notice the peculiar aesthetic that is all its own. There is a mode of performance that is all about casualness. It only means to say, 'look, this is easy and painless', but it has the effect of looking like magic morphing into the everyday. So a blonde in cowboy boots and gold bikini types while she sits on her own head; Meribeth Old, a 1950s star and the queen of this 'dazzling but wifely' idiom, leans on her elbows with her legs in the air and primly sips tea; in another photograph, she is making a cake with her ankles wrapped around her back. Coney Island may have had its heyday in the twenties but contortion could make a comeback – at the circus or in an art gallery – any time.

Gaby Wood

http://www.pinhole.com

Pinhole photography, descended from the camera obscura, can claim to be the most archaic means of mechanical image production. Euclid demonstrated the principles of pinhole optics some 2,300 years ago, and Leonardo perfected the camera obscura as a copying device in the 16th century, bequeathing it to generations of artists trying to ensure the verisimilitude of their paintings.

The camera obscura – literally, a dark room – replicates the workings of the human eye. A minuscule aperture concentrates the passage of light from a fiercely illuminated world into an inner, dark chamber, where, traversing a lens or some sort of convex glass, the rays of light reform into a perfect image of the external scene inside the chamber, albeit upside down. By the age of enlightenment, the camera obscura had proliferated and made the art of portraiture available to everyone. High street shops housed huge models, actual rooms that the painter entered in order to trace the image of the sitter, which was projected on to ground glass plates by a series of lenses and mirrors. Then came Daguerre, who sensitised the plates with silver salts, completing the transformation of the camera into an automaton, in which images recorded themselves. The physical image captured inside the camera obscura had become, by 1837, a permanent chemical impression.

Perhaps it is possible to imagine the impact of those early images: the excitement felt by their first witnesses at a magical transformation which moved and duplicated reality across space and time; their astonishment at how a pinprick-sized hole situated between light and dark could replicate the world upside down, allowing what was outside a blind wall to be seen with perfect clarity inside.

Pinhole photography, as a result of its necessarily long exposures, tends to age its subjects, to apply a patina of history indiscriminately to every scene. Human figures become ghostly emanations, and architecture – a favoured subject since it tends to stand still – devolves into monumental volumes realised in slightly skewed perspectives. To look at pinhole photographs now is to appreciate the subtle tactility of an anachronistic technology – the ever-so-delicate binding of the real into a fragile surface, as contingent, rapid and ineffable as a skilled watercolour.

Like the camera obscura in its day, the internet is a medium of marvel as it casts images across time and space at a speed faster than even Leonardo could have imagined. Yet to view the virtual galleries of two websites devoted to pinhole photography (www.pinhole.org and www.pinhole.com) is to become aware of the mismarriage of the two media, of how much is lost in the process of digital reproduction, as the subtle distortions and physicalities of the pinhole image, resulting from the play of light, time, movement and chemical event, are levelled and erased in the homogenous pixellation of the image. Mysterious ectoplasm becomes cleaned-up digital blur, summoned at the press of a button.

The marvellous alchemy of early photography – the passage from negative to positive, from top to bottom, from dark to light – seems fundamentally incompatible with a digital medium which dissipates the relationship between original reality and photographic image, and does away with traditional time and space. The camera obscura as specular and spatial metaphor has consistently inspired some of civilisation's most important thinkers – and for the metaphoric richness of the device, I'd recommend Sarah Kofman's fascinating *Camera Obscura of Ideology* (Athlone Press 1998), rather than the enthusiastic amateurism of the practical pinholers to be found on the websites (with the possible exception of Ben Conrad's endearing, fetishistic all-over pinhole body suit at www.pinhole.com).

Marx, for example, recognised that something rather peculiar happened inside the dark space of the camera obscura. While the image created inside the camera appeared to be the most objective rendering of reality conceivable, it was at the same time, different, in being inverted, obscured and separated from the real. For Marx, this interior world was ghostly, fantastic, phantasmagoric, even fetishistic. (Interestingly, Kofman also tells us that the camera obscura, as a term, originated in the medieval monastery to describe a dark, secret place where monks who could no longer bear the privations of the regime were permitted to indulge temporarily in all things transgressive.) Marx invoked the camera obscura as a metaphor to elucidate the illogical workings of ideology in the minds of men – how we fall prey to distorting systems of belief, such as religion and morality, while believing them to be natural and real. Freud also exploited photography and the light-tight room as an image to communicate his theories of the unconscious. He described the unconscious as a dark antechamber, in which a myriad psychic phenomena were housed and filed – like photographic negatives waiting to be developed. At the threshold, in the place of the pinhole, between the dark room and a second narrower room – a kind of drawing room – stands a watchman or censor, whose job it is to decide which of these unconscious drives will pass over the threshold from the darkness of the camera obscura into the light of the camera lucida – that is, human consciousness.

Despite its metaphoric richness, and its enduring popular appeal, pinhole photography is used by very few contemporary artists to interesting effect. The notable exception is, of course, Steven Pippin who, like Marx and Freud, clearly understands the connection between the everyday and the marvellous as mediated in the camera obscura. Among seminal Pippin works realised in launderettes is his ER (a personal tribute to Muybridge's pseudo-scientific photographs, which have been partially discredited by his seemingly endless studies of women getting in and out of bed), a meditation on photography, process and posing in which the artist, working alone at night, is photographed repeatedly by a row of 100 pinhole-adapted washing machines while walking past with an erection. The resulting images are then put through the wash-and-spin cycle of the machine to be developed and processed as photographs.

Kate Bush

homestudio.thing.net is a site run by French composer and musician Jerome Joy, based in Nice. At the start, you see a sketch of someone sitting in front of a computer screen. That means, you see someone in the same position and doing the same thing that you are doing. It's a nice welcome, a light reflection of the medium and the working process it demands: sitting alone at a desk, hands on the keys, eyes on the screen. But this site is not concerned with a critique of the computer age, nor with exploring the frontiers of the internet, although critical aspects such as these are not excluded as you click through. The main topic of this site is music and its status and role in an era in which the producing, receiving and distributing of it are changing radically.

The smoothly programmed and understated design of the site offers the possibility to experience various kinds of audio-visual experiments, some of them interactive. Most are created by Joy himself or are contributed by other artists; some are documentaries of pieces performed at concerts or exhibitions. The most interesting part of the site, for me at least, is the so-called 'forum hub', which was started in October 1999.

'forum hub' is a place for discussion, introduced by a lengthy essay by Joy in which he summarises some thoughts on contemporary music. He sums up by posing some questions and inviting people to answer. Joy is concerned, for example, with the role of the live concert – whether it is an adequate form in which to present music today. He is also concerned with the possibility the internet offers in terms of 'an extension of electronic and electroacoustic practices'.

One can follow a lively discussion of these and other related topics. Along the way, contributors give hints about their backgrounds and their works (some are musicians and composers with international reputations in the field of experimental music). Bernhard Guenther explains his concept of 'sound painting', describing his way of manipulating a sound with different programmes to arrive at something comparable to the layering of colour on canvas. The British composer Rhys Chatham speaks of a 'golden age' that he believes music-makers are experiencing now. His positive thinking is based on the fact that compositions today can easily cross the borders of genres.

This last point is the subject of a critique by other contributors. Chatham has to concede that a hard rock band that expands the borders of the genre in which it works will be made well aware of these borders, in the form of beer cans thrown on to the stage by a crowd who continue to observe the laws of the genre.

That is just one point of a discussion that is still running. At a time when the internet is increasingly being used as a distribution canal for contemporary music (through mail order shops and MP3), such a discussion is an important step.

Martin Pesch

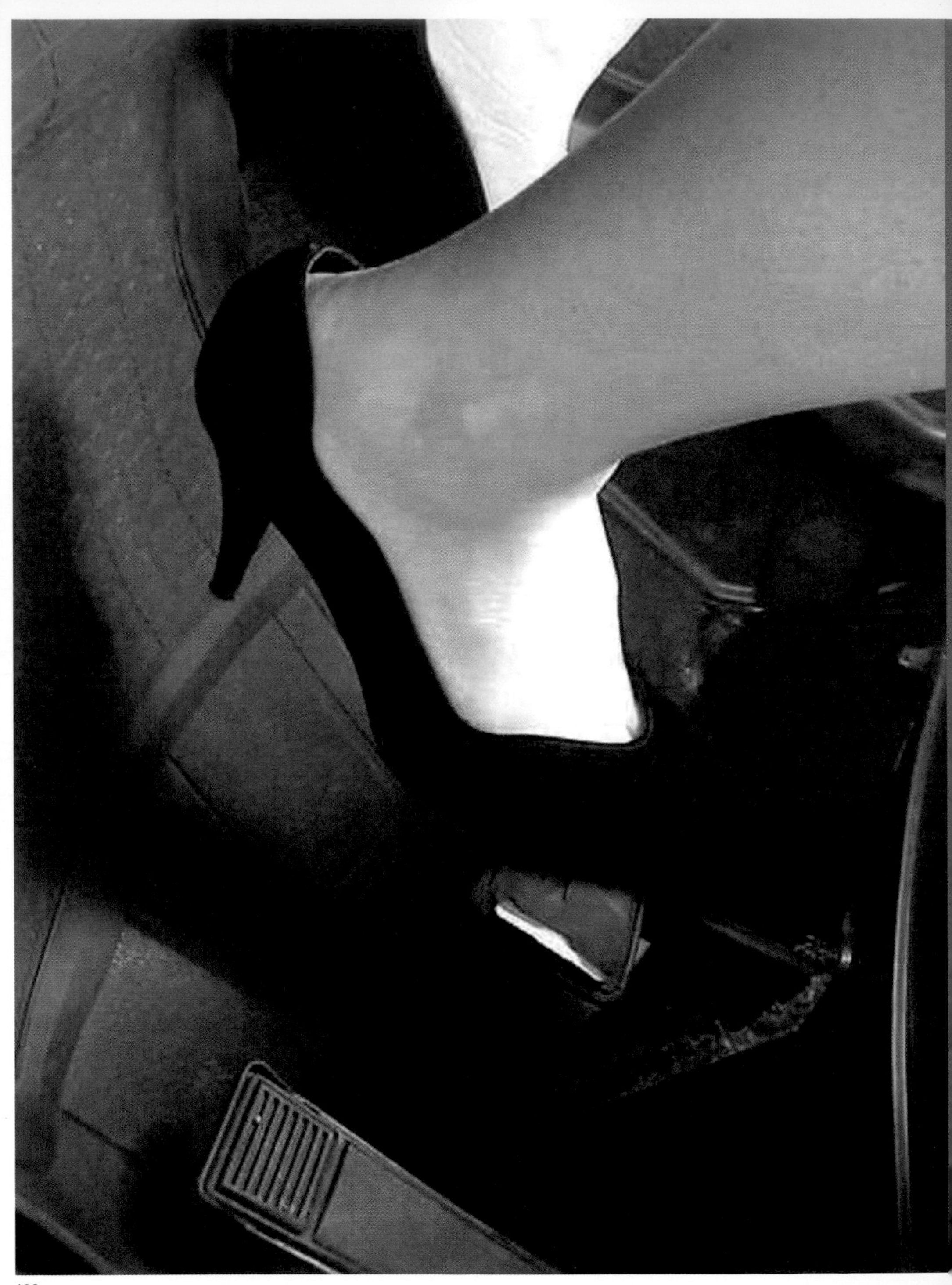

Tiffany-Anne is the sexiest revver around. No one can rotate her foot on the gas pedal and get that Dodge Durango to fire like Tiffany. Wearing nothing other than pale blue stilettos with six-inch heels and an ankle chain, she can keep a revving scene going for a good twenty minutes. All Cory knows is, he sure does wish he was that gas pedal.

Cory is the brains, and from what I have heard, the stonewashed jeans, behind pedalextreme.com, a web site for guys with a foot fetish whose thing is images of women's feet pressing down on the accelerator.

It's not that specialised, I mean, it's OK for their feet to be propped up on the steering wheel sometimes, or they could be stepping in and out of a car, or 'cranking over a flooded clunker'. There are barefoot fans of Pedal Power, sneakers and sock fans, and an insatiable demand for snakeskin stilettos. The PP community idolise feet that enjoy home pedicures and lightly chipped nail varnish, toe rings and can cope with six-inch heels and a tight ankle chain, but would be lost in a Prada mule. If a girl wants to be a Pedal Power model, it seems she has to decide whether she wants to be either a starter, a cranker, a flooder or a revver of a car that might have been on blocks in the trailer park for some time.

Sometimes the guys post messages saying they want to beat up a car for giving the ladies a hard time, but mostly they quite like it. Don't get me wrong, they treat women with respect on pedal extreme.com, but they respect a car just a little bit more.

Gentlemen of the road, they like nothing better than finding a woman leaning over the bonnet, helplessly running her hands through her high-lighted hair, or pleading with a flooded clunker with maroon upholstery. One day he might be a garage mechanic just passing with a very big truck, or a lucky hitchhiker.

Sitting next to Kellie or Cindy or Silkyfeet, they watch as she tries to start the Chevy Eldorado in vain. Maybe it would help if she took her white stilettos off, but that doesn't ever seem to occur to them. 'I'll let ya in on a little secret,' wrote Cory. 'Some of Silkyfeet's revving sequences will nail you to the floor. Pretending you are the pedal, lying there watching her drive is a pretty damn good treat.'

Catherine Wilson

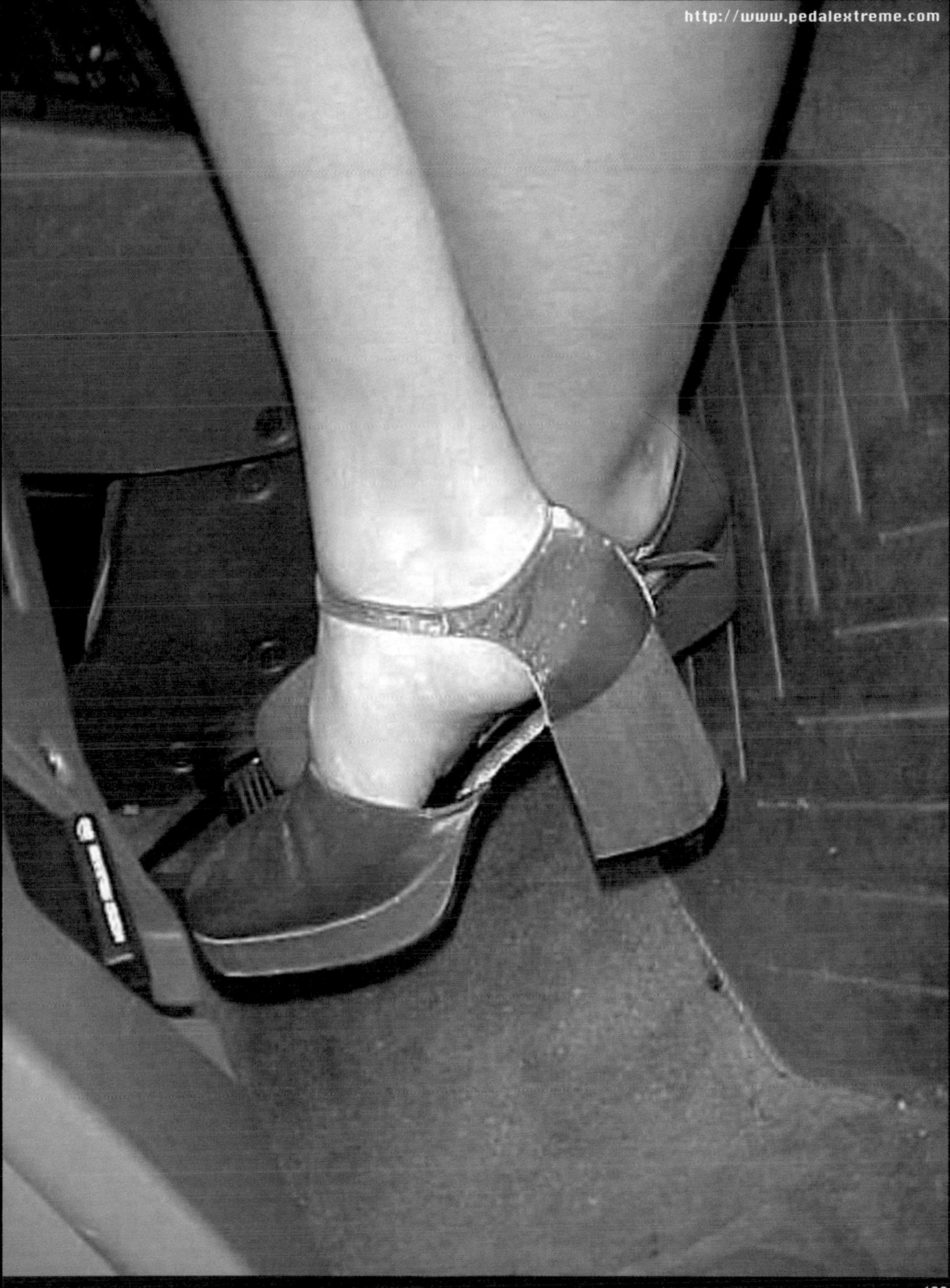

Back in the days when sex was dirty, masturbation was a disreputable activity, performed in furtive solitude, in the full and fearful expectation that at any moment the eyeballs might implode, the penis erupt in green lesions, and a posse of priests and headmasters enter the room wielding torches, even axes. What fun it was.

Today, masturbation is a guiltless, sanitised activity, conducted in an atmosphere of amiable fraternisation, while jolly, well-meaning experts peer over the shoulder offering advice. 'Have you tried the Reverse Scrotum Grab?', 'Why not make a vagina out of inflatable armbands stuck together with Krazy Glue?', 'Consider heating up the melon first...' Masturbation has become a participation sport – not part of its original remit.

There is no more convincing evidence of this than JackinWorld, a website devoted to the explication and de-mystification of self-pleasure. Describing itself as the ultimate masturbation resource, JackinWorld contains an embarrassment of statistics and information about the subject, from its misty Sumerian beginnings to its many sticky endings, all meticulously catalogued by a team of enthusiasts that, we are told blithely, has a total of 25,000 masturbations under its belt, or not under its belt, as the case may be.

If this ejaculatory legacy doesn't make you gag, then the page of 'masturbation humor' should do the trick (best example: 'sorry I'm late for work, I had to help my Uncle Jack off the horse') a highlight of which is the Masturbata Song, sung to the tune of the Macarena. Surveys, tips and lists of FAQs are threaded together with all the pseudo-sociability the web can muster. A page titled Jackin for Her introduces us to the charms of electric toothbrushes and stuffed bears. Site visitors of both sexes discuss techniques, as though swapping cake recipes.

It makes the mind boggle, but not the trousers. jackinworld.com is strictly non-pornographic. It has fewer dirty pictures than *Jackanory*. In fact, cleanliness is an obsession. The bonus of a method that requires the testicles to be hooked over the edge of the bathroom basin is the proximity of the faucet for easy clean-up. The average person who reads JackinWorld, we are told, is male, 14–15 years old and has masturbated once or twice a day since he was 11, mainly using the fist grip and using spit as a 'lube'. Why anyone with that much experience should need a guide like this is beyond me. Treating sex as just another commercially ubiquitous, squeaky-clean commodity has its dangers. Many young people have turned to drugs instead, unable to face agony aunts advising on the eventuality of passing wind during cunnilingus, or explaining how to insert strings of beads in the bottom. They have to find their thrills somewhere.

'Wouldn't it be great', declares jackinworld.com, 'if every teenager could masturbate and be free to make the same amount of noise as if he were playing a video game?' No. It would be the end of the world as we know it.

Martin Plimmer

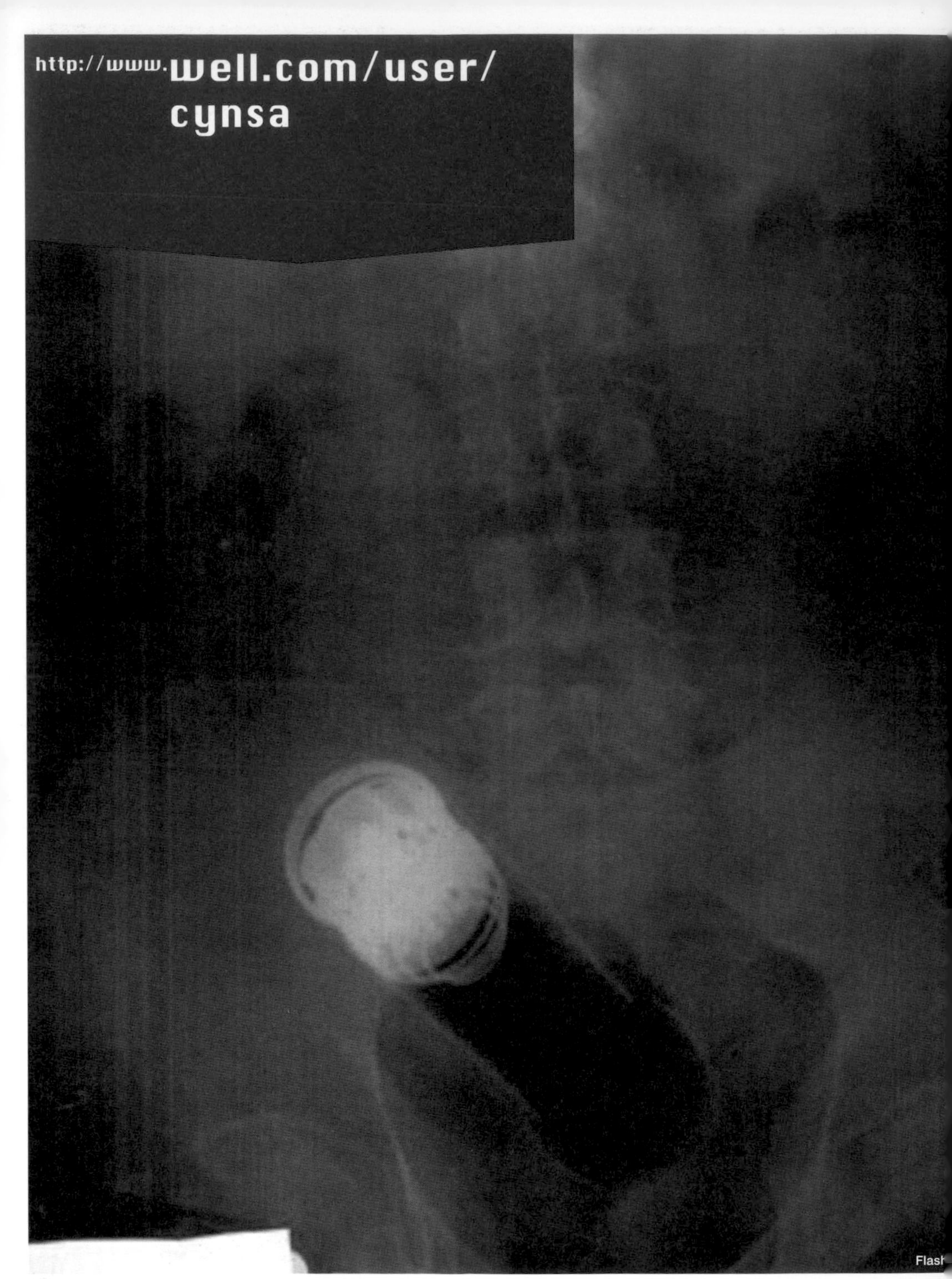
http://www.well.com/user/
cynsa

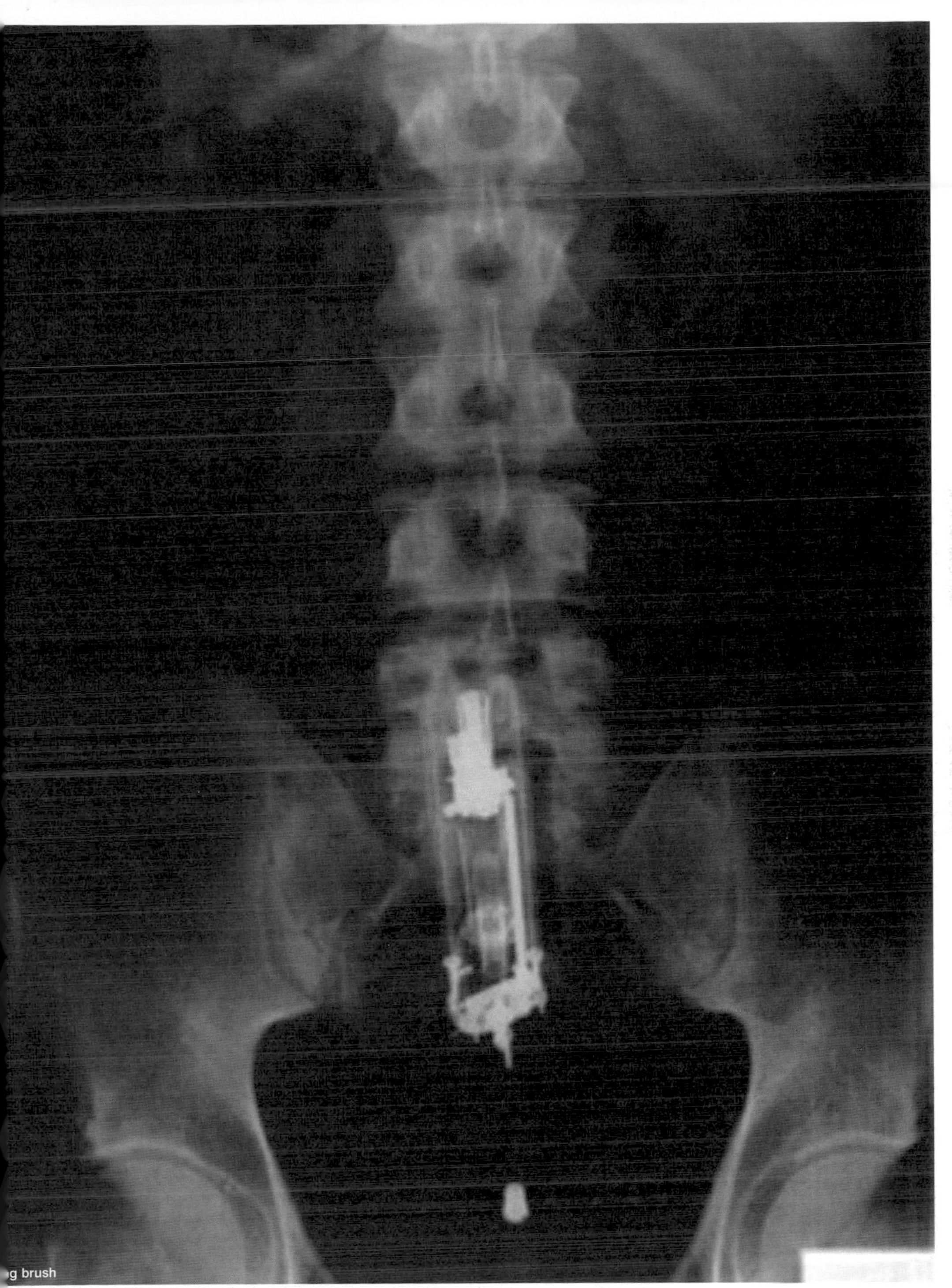

g brush

http://www.well.com/user/cynsa

It's a simple idea, trawling the medical literature for examples of a specific, very comic problem. And it's undoubtedly effective. These case studies, for instance, have given me the impression that there can be no finer or more cheering event for a busy casualty department than the arrival of a man – and it generally is a man – complaining of rectal pain. Things'll get pretty gross, it's true, but still there seems something generous, public-spirited, in his appearance. The way the atmosphere must lift. Doctors, nurses, anaesthetists – their eyes light up, their bodies shake slightly with suppressed hysteria. They try to remain straightfaced, but their minds are racing.

How embarassed is he, this new patient? He's very embarrassed. How long has it taken him to pluck up the courage to come in? A couple of days, a week; my God, maybe a month. And what explanation has he managed to come up with in all that time? He had a bet with a friend. He was fooling around. Or, the immortal formula, he was having a shower and slipped.

At last, they say to themselves as they take him off for an x-ray. After all the stories they've heard, after all their colleagues' jokes... At last they've come face to face... No, I'll start again.

At last they're going to be dealing with their very own case of 'a self-inserted, unusual rectal foreign body'.

'Unusual'. It is ironic touches like this that show how much medics relish these unpredictable little reminders of the richness of the human imagination. 'Unusual'. When people set their hearts on putting stuff up their arses, the sky, basically, is the limit. They have preferences, naturally. The contents of the fruit bowl. Anything tool-shaped. Glass things – a buttock-clenchingly varied range of glass things. 100-watt bulbs. Peanut butter jars.

But that still leaves a fair amount of room for self-expression. One man turned up with a pair of spectacles, a suitcase key, a tobacco pouch and a magazine on board. Another, by letting his boyfriend give him a concrete enema, executed a very personal homage to Rachel Whiteread.

The hapless, slapstick humour of these scenarios of course appeals as much to doctors as it does to the website's visitors. Who could be unmoved by the 64-year-old who 'in an attempt to ease his constipation, had inserted a microwave egg boiler (MEB) into his rectum'. But the other great attraction, from a professional point of view, of rectal foreign bodies is that they are a fantastic technical challenge. Getting an MEB in – all 11cm in diameter at its widest point – is one thing. But getting it out? So the reports move swiftly on. It's down to work and, goodness, these doctors rise to the occasion. Foley catheters with inflated balloons, nurse! Try the lithotomy position. No? Trendelenburg! And, the *coup de théâtre*, the forceps – spong, Blacks tissue – until, with their obstretric variants, the perfect 'delivery' is performed. Every one of these mini-dramas, it's a pleasure to say, ends happily. No complications. 24 hours of observation. And then an offer of psychological counselling, jauntily made and jauntily declined.

All of this is, as the website compilers say, 'muchly amusing'. And popular – over 30 million visits in under three years. The unashamed tackiness of it only jars when you get to the feeble, self-authored stuff about butts in general. At this point, readers of Jean-Luc Hennig's book, *The Rear View. A brief and elegant history of bottoms through the ages* (Souvenir Press, London 1995) will rebel.

Ah no, my friends, they will say. The derrière is a complex, rich subject, too long shrouded in shame and embarrassment. A list of ways some people block it, and others clear it, can never do it justice. Where is the poetry, the tenderness, the metaphysics? Where is Salvador Dali, who said that 'it is through the behind that the greatest mysteries can be fathomed' and who personally found a 'significant similarity between the buttocks of one of my female guests at Port Lligat and the four-dimension or space-time continuum that I call the four-buttock continuum, that is, the atom'. Such visitors – French, perhaps – will not, I'm afraid, be satisfied.

Will Hobson

http://members.xoom.com/castroom/pop

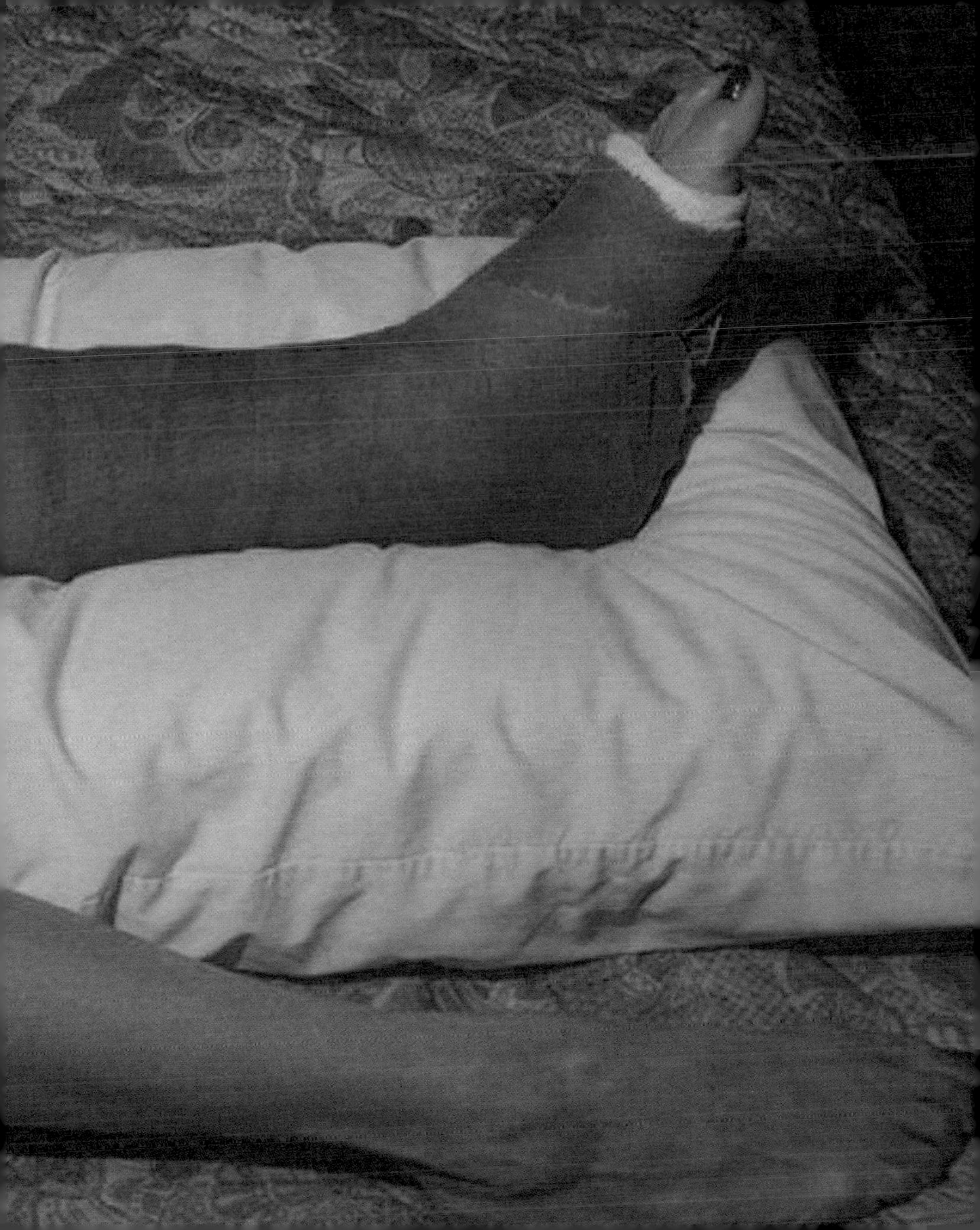

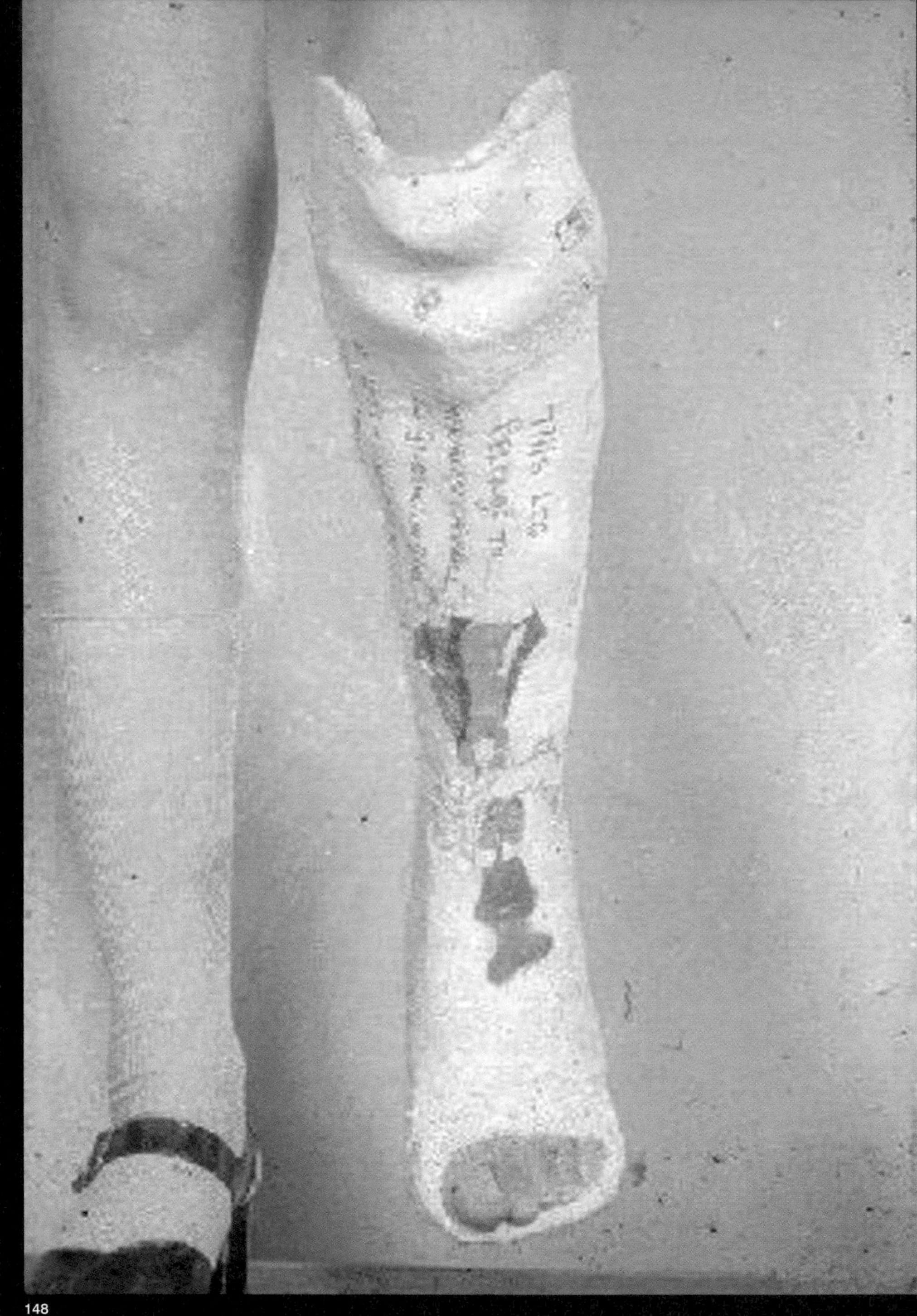

http://members.xoom.com/castroom/pop

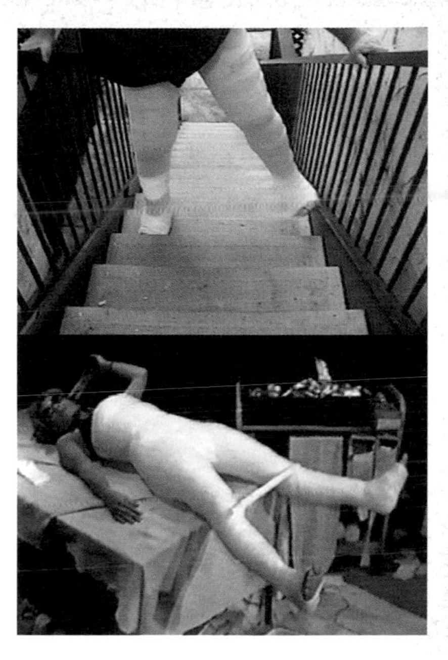

The internet is for people who lack the flair (and face) for conversation. They need monologues and masks, because they know in everyday life their attempts at discussion will be returned to sender. In the old days, such people might find a useful purpose as morris dancers, potters, or basket weavers – they might pass fruitful months, even lifetimes trying to fit matchstick galleons into empty beer bottles. Now they are redeemed. They can lock themselves in darkened rooms in Streatham and interface with their home computer. The sun comes up, the sun goes down, the planets sail across the sky and it must be *somebody's* fault. It is no way for a grown man to behave.

Doesn't everyone show symptoms of 'Dolly's Knicker Disease'? Give a little boy a Barbie and the first thing he does is upend her to carry out an inspection of her bottom. The first thing a teenager does left alone in a female boudoir is rummage through her lingerie, select the laciest pieces, wack them on, then wack off in front of the mirror. So isn't it obvious what a grown man will do when left alone with a computer? He will log on to any site of sex, sin or perversion. With the mouse in one hand and an erection the size of a small mammal in the other he will erupt screens of cyber-spunk over any fe-mail. This, as you may well have guessed, is precisely what I did. Like my beauty to the mirror, I turned straight to the weirdest reflection of my warped personality I could find – disasters in plaster. The castroom site shows pictures of people who derive a weird sexual satisfaction encasing their perfectly healthy limbs in casts. Actually, some of them would have looked quite attractive if they had cut their heads off. I do have experience of being in plaster. Some years ago, I parachuted out of an aeroplane while stoned. As I hit the ground, I felt my leg snap in two like a sap branch. As I lay prostrate, the ambulance speeding towards me, I thought to myself 'at last something has happened to me'. At last I am cast in the leading role. Being a cripple is a bit like being an old age pensioner – it is a career in which even the most hopeless cannot fail.

If only those internet natterers would log on to this site and learn their lesson, lopping off their pointless enthusiasms as these perverts have learned to restrain their useless limbs. If only they were believers in Beckettian silence, instead of practitioners of interminable cyberbabble. If only they would remember that in cyberspace everyone can hear you scream – the noise is deafening. Then they would regain the atavistic art of conversation. After all, speech is only the small change of silence.

Sebastian Horsley

http://www.2ndhandsmokeinc.com

This is a site devoted to men with a fetish for cigarettes and 'dedicated to the imagery of women smoking'; it goes beyond those overplayed jokes about All the President's Cigars. Here, in brief, are the things to do with cigarettes that the Chief Medical Officer didn't think about when he issued the Government Health Warning. Forget the dangers of passive smoking or the wayward pleasure of a post-coital drag, this is full-frontal Freud, unpacking and literalising the symbolic meanings of a ciggy.

In case the surfer is in any doubt, a picture library and free video clips reinforce the point. Viewers can even join a new VIP Club. Aja, Angela, Babette, Eden and Gina perform on screen. Puffable dildos are rolled between ballooning breasts (simulating the delight of a connoisseur handling a virgin Havana), or sucked provocatively like a lollipop while the women touch themselves. The smoking props make the women vulnerable and aggressive by turn, as the cigarettes are transformed into a baby's dummy or some macho accoutrement, the metonymic substitution for the silent community of male voyeurs that is consuming online.

There's something disingenuous about the conflation of cigarette and penis, mouth and sex that the site promotes. More than a nod and a wink, this is a sledgehammer that knocks the point into a platitude, ironing out sexiness into an explicit spectacle. In the process, the viewer is directed how to read that moment in the movies when the protagonist's eyes glaze over and the heroine finally lights up. The glowing tip of the cigarette stands in for the hero's burning passion; the heroine's deep inhalations are demonstrative of the profound sexual cravings that aren't permitted on screen. If you didn't get the message, 2ndhandsmokeinc.com is here to remind you that cigarettes mean sex – serious sex.

And there are people out there who like to hear it. Men like Matt and Darren, who share their views in the 'Smoke Talk' chat-room about the eroticism of women who use cigarette holders, the man with a fixation on smoke-rings, or the self-styled French 'inhaler' who is searching for British women 'who love nothing more than French inhaling huge cigars'. It's at moments like this that 2ndhandsmokeinc.com begins to read like a self-parody, ridiculing the fetish it purports to celebrate.

This is a curiously one-sided site from which the tough, leather face of the Marlboro Man has been conspicuously banned. Even though it may be true that men are giving up smoking, while proportionally more women are taking it up, what about the imagery of men smoking? The hard-man detective tossing the cigarette out of his mouth as he begins the chase, Clint Eastwood chewing on the butt of a cigarillo, the intellectual chain smoker, or Churchill's cigary profile? Like the traces of a cigarette in an ashtray which signals the passage of the criminal in the detective plot, the cigarettes and cigars that pervade the pictures of 2ndhandsmokeinc.com are signs of the absent man who has already been, but who may yet return. As such, they are signs of the times.

Shannan Peckham

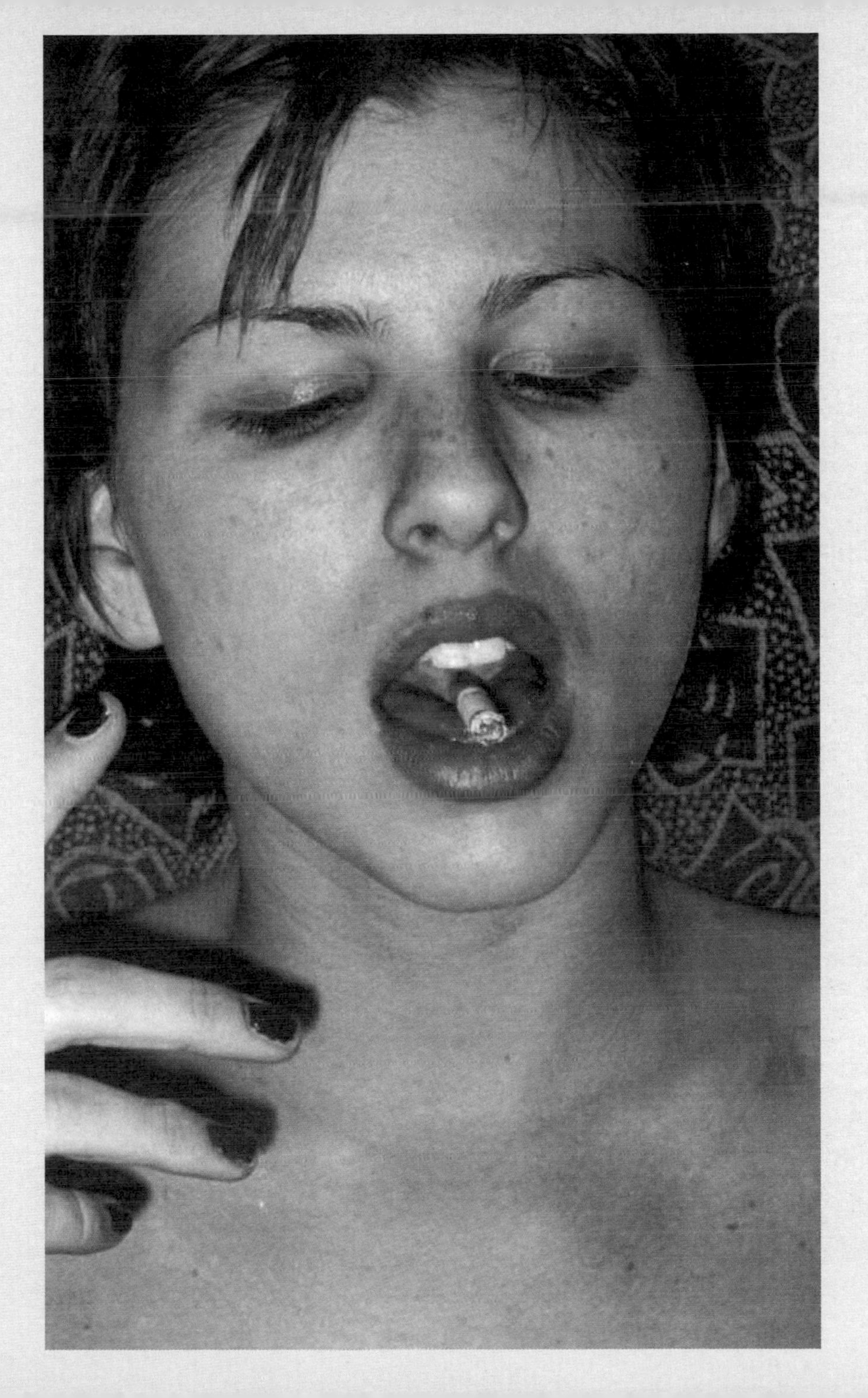

http://members.xoom.com/MrBlowup/xblow.html

http://members.xoom.com/MrBlowup/xblow.html

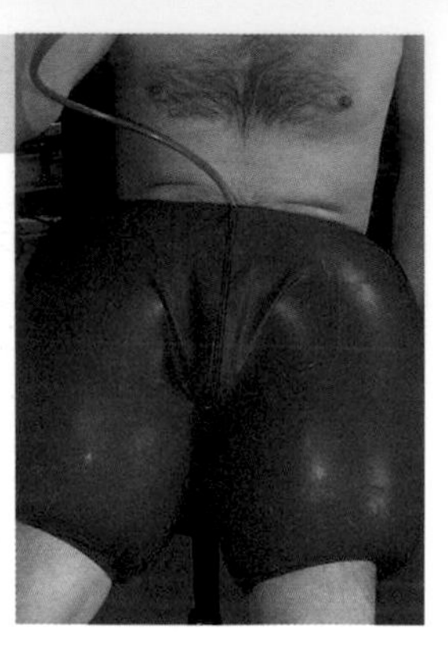

Mr Blowup is a 45-year-old fetishist whose greatest joy in life is the touch of rubber. That, in itself, is unremarkable. The fact that *Skin Two* is now as familiar a magazine title as *The Face* and *Elle Decoration* is ample proof that lovers of latex are all around us. But Mr Blowup displays a devotion to his materials that transcends the nether world of thigh boots, jumpsuits and face masks. The man is an artist, an experimenter, a suburban Leigh Bowery whose pumped-up costumes distend the human form – or, sometimes, encase it so completely that it is reduced to mere stuffing.

Mr Blowup explains himself in an introductory essay. As a child, of course, he was drawn to the smoothness of rubber and latex, but it was inflatable toys and paddling pools in particular that excited him. The thrill of inflation is that the body is squeezed all over and restrained, he explains.

Few of his girlfriends understood his hobby until he met his current love – let's call her Mrs Blowup: he does – who now appears in his photographs and supervises the more technically challenging (and potentially life-threatening) tableaux.

There are 13 galleries of photographs within Mr Blowup's well ordered site. Sometimes, he is alone; sometimes, touchingly, Mrs Blowup is propped up beside him on the sofa, next to the rubber plant, she in inflatable black (you can tell it's her from the inflatable breast area), he in fetching, inflatable red.

Some of the strangest scenes – also the purest and, let's be honest, the funniest – are in Gallery 8, where Mr B is so subordinate to his second skin that he becomes an inflatable black lozenge, limbless and eyeless. Leaning against the wall in the hall of his home 'outside London', as if he were a roll of rubber flooring that had just been delivered by Pickfords. The only blemish on this living sculpture is the point at which the air hose exits the rubber and snakes away towards the front room. He will restrain himself further still if the means permit. His 'inflatable womb' requires that he curl himself up in the middle of a latex ball, and in other pictures he reduces himself to the size and shape of a bin bag. Suburbia pervades Mr Blowup's photographs: a pine curtain rail here, a section of B&Q fencing there. And Mr B likes his house. In fact he is torn between his desire to spend money making his own rubber confections (he currently buys them off the peg and customises them) and the need to keep the house and car maintained.

But in the end, the house must come second. The man has a calling. And, possibly, floorspace awaiting him in the Tate.

Richard Preston

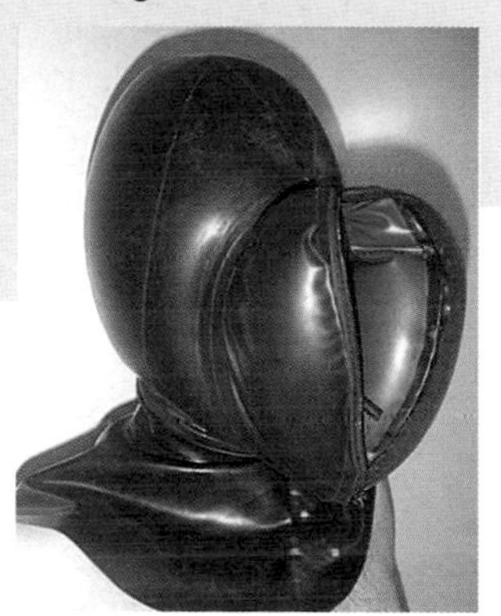

http://members.xoom.com/MrBlowup/xblow.html

http://www.wowwow.co.uk

If you have a website to recommend for review
please e-mail: editor@wowwow.co.uk

EXECUTIVE EDITORS AND DESIGN
Miles Murray Sorrell (FUEL)
www.fuel-design.com

EDITOR
Richard Preston

CONTRIBUTING EDITORS
Jethro Marshall
Matthew Donaldson

Wow Wow
PO BOX 24873
London E1 6FP

The views expressed in this book are those of the individual writers and do not necessarily represent the views of Wow Wow Ltd.

Every effort has been made to contact the sites reviewed to obtain their permission for publication. We apologise to those we could not contact.

Thank you to all the writers for their contributions and to the sites for permission to publish their pictures.

Published in 2000 by Laurence King Publishing
an imprint of Calmann & King Ltd

71 Great Russell Street
London WC1B 3BN
Tel: +44 20 7831 6351
Fax: +44 20 7831 8356
e-mail: enquiries@calmann-king.co.uk
www.laurence-king.com

A catalogue record for this book is available from the British Library.

ISBN 1 85669 207 8

Printed in Italy